IMPRESSIONS OF AN INVASION

who were suffering from cabin fever while being unable to travel overseas.

I had an urge to shout out how Georgia was available for tourism during the pandemic – everyone could cast aside their reservations about vaccinations and quarantines. Alas I am unable to convince others to overcome their phobias of getting infected.

Having gone through a variety of social distancing measures in several highly populated cities in Asia, I was truly grateful for the personal space bubbles of the European lifestyles. The pavements, restaurants, parks and attractions were not as overcrowded with people most of the time and anyone with a car would be dispersing outwards from the urbanised centres over the weekends. All we had to do was to minimise the time we spent inside any public indoor arenas and stay away from places of interest during festivals.

Ukrainians have a rich tradition of celebrating festivals. We have been passing from one party to another, celebrating the New Year on 1st January, then the Orthodox Christmas, the Old New Year in accordance with the Gregorian calendar, the Chinese Lunar New Year, Valentine's day, *Yuan Xiao* (the first full moon in the lunisolar new year) and towards the end of February, we were making preparations for the pancakes party for the upcoming Masnytsia festival.

Progressing alongside the festivals were the ever increasing build-up of Russian armed forces along the Northern, Eastern and Southern borders of Ukraine. They had been accumulating their forces under the pretence of large scale military exercises even though a huge number of Russian forces were in Belarus.

IX SHEN

Top: Feeling casual and carefree during COVID, we stayed away from crowded places.

Bottom: Swinging chair for two without the Charleston

Making Hay

TRYING TO STAY alive inside a war zone is insane. Our strongest companions for sanity are tasks and thoughts.

When I recollect how I felt when I watched those black and white documentary footage of people doing the Charleston during the decade of decadence before the impending Second World War, I never fully understood how could they have been so carefree, because those scenes would immediately cut into the chaos of battle. But as a viewer, I knew what was going to happen while they did not. Now whenever I look at my holiday footage, which I had been preparing to post online before the onslaught of the invasion, I feel paradoxically remorseful.

Like many people, I also believed that it was impossible for imperial expansion to be occurring in this century. But by now most of us have adapted and accepted the inevitability of the Russian invasion of Ukraine. Between the impossible and the inevitable was the crisis which we tried to survive.

In early February 2022, my wife Natalia and I had just returned to Kyiv after a wonderful trip to the Caucasus mountains. We were still joyous from the experience of being able to travel, snowboard and party after two years of COVID restrictions. Our exhilarations to be liberated from lockdowns were so overwhelming that I felt guilty for many of my friends

Idyllic social distancing inside a coffee cabin up in the mountains

THE FIRST WEEK

We can detect the trembling in the voice of a nervous speaker or the stuttering of a panicking person. But having a tremor or stutter in a form of writing is difficult to enact. Because some of the errors which were typed out rapidly when I recalled the accompanying emotions of that particular moment would be corrected as a typo or adjusted for better reading. With nostalgia, I yearn for those ribbon typewriters which captures the reality of each moment, as the varied inked intensities of the typefaces would fluctuate in parallel with my anxiety.

There were many moments that we survived through the invasion that I am unable to rank them in any ascending or descending order. I dread answering questions that asks what I felt was the "most" about anything – for at every moment, I was just grateful to have survived.

So I decided that writing my experience in chronological order, and as realistic to my emotions during each moment, would be the fairest manner for me to recount the chain of events.

Like Homer Simpson facing the anxiety of death, I was constantly pin-balling through the stages of denial, anger, fear, bargaining and acceptance. The writing is honest to the experience and will at times behave like a pinball trapped among bumpsters, rattling to reflect the excitement of the narrative.

For when normalcy is ambiguous, sanity becomes subjective.

A NOTE FROM THE AUTHOR

I finally understood what it meant to be shell-shocked when I was immobilised while in midstride by the shock wave of an artillery blast that swept past me.

Although my body remained unharmed, my sense of logic and reasoning went offline. My fight or flight response was triggered with adrenaline charged in all cylinders. But the nearest bunker was too far away for a flight and the attackers were not in visual range for a fight. I was mind-blown by the shock of the shelling.

The only respite for me was to switch into metacognition mode by mentally escaping elsewhere, while my body behaved like a statue.

I had hoped to record everything I was seeing, hearing, smelling and feeling – each thought that flashed through my mind and the consequential imagination that had been spurred.

Being caught up by the invasion of Kyiv is what we call in the film-making business, a fish out of water scenario. Other than using the phrase as an expression, we tend to overlook how traumatic it was for the fish as it tries to survive. How much effort and hope are placed into each flip or the despair and fear overcome with every flop.

CONTENTS

A Note from the Author 7

The First Week 9

The Second Week 71

The Third Week 129

Afterword 221

About the Author 231

© 2023 Ix Shen

Published in 2023 by Marshall Cavendish Editions
An imprint of Marshall Cavendish International

All rights reserved

No part of this publication may be reproduced, stored in a retrieval system or transmitted, in any form or by any means, electronic, mechanical, photocopying, recording or otherwise, without the prior permission of the copyright owner. Requests for permission should be addressed to the Publisher, Marshall Cavendish International (Asia) Private Limited, 1 New Industrial Road, Singapore 536196. Tel: (65) 6213 9300 E-mail: genref@sg.marshallcavendish.com
Website: www.marshallcavendish.com

The publisher makes no representation or warranties with respect to the contents of this book, and specifically disclaims any implied warranties or merchantability or fitness for any particular purpose, and shall in no event be liable for any loss of profit or any other commercial damage, including but not limited to special, incidental, consequential, or other damages.

Other Marshall Cavendish Offices:
Marshall Cavendish Corporation, 800 Westchester Ave, Suite N-641, Rye Brook, NY 10573, USA • Marshall Cavendish International (Thailand) Co Ltd, 253 Asoke, 16th Floor, Sukhumvit 21 Road, Klongtoey Nua, Wattana, Bangkok 10110, Thailand • Marshall Cavendish (Malaysia) Sdn Bhd, Times Subang, Lot 46, Subang Hi-Tech Industrial Park, Batu Tiga, 40000 Shah Alam, Selangor Darul Ehsan, Malaysia

Marshall Cavendish is a registered trademark of Times Publishing Limited

National Library Board, Singapore Cataloguing in Publication Data
Name(s): Shen, Ix.
Title: Impressions of an invasion : a correspondent in Ukraine / Ix Shen.
Description: Singapore : Marshall Cavendish Editions, 2023.
Identifier(s): ISBN 978-981-5113-35-8
Subject(s): LCSH: Shen, Ix. | Ukraine--History--Russian Invasion, 2022---
　　　　Personal narratives. | Singaporeans--Ukraine. | Kyïv (Ukraine)--
　　　　History--21st century. | Kyïv (Ukraine)--Biography.
Classification: DDC 947.7086092--dc23

Printed in Singapore

IMPRESSIONS OF AN INVASION

A CORRESPONDENT IN UKRAINE

Ix Shen

Opposite page: Andriivskyi Descent – wide, open and historic.

Left: Beauty of seasonal transitions

Bottom: Traditional Christmas fair at the Square of Contracts

It was not much of a concern as the Russian forces had been repeating such military manoeuvres almost annually.

But no one in Ukraine was naïve enough to believe that the Russians were only conducting military exercises. After the swift and abrupt military annexation of the Crimea peninsular following the exodus of Ukraine ex-president Yanukovich, who fled in disgrace in 2014, everyone understood that the Kremlin's rhetoric had to be taken with a large clump of salt.

For the past eight years, the war for Donbas in eastern Ukraine had been raging. Many believed that the current military build up would be a classic strategy to "attack west by rousing east" or 声东击西. Therefore, no one was surprised when Russia announced its recognition of the independence of the newly founded states.

Similarly, no one panicked when the Russian tanks crossed the eastern borders into Ukraine. The only change was that from that moment, all hostile troops situated inside Ukraine then had to wear insignias identifying their country.

Despite the closures of many foreign embassies and exodus of the affluent people with their assets causing the free-fall of the Ukrainian currency, the general consensus of the local folks was resolute in standing their ground.

If the Russians wanted to die on foreign soil, then so be it.

Shattering of Peace

THE INVASION OF Ukraine officially began on February 24th. However for me the peace was shattered on the night of 23rd.

That night is etched into my memory, when I stood on my balcony sipping my *teh tarik* after another inconclusive discussion with my wife about whether we should leave or stay. I was staring into the night sky with my mind still processing the pros and cons about manoeuvring in the midst of a military conflict, COVID pandemic restrictions, inflation and what nots, when I saw a circular flash in the sky.

The speed of its disappearance from the sky made me wonder if the moon had been rapidly covered by fast moving clouds because

Traits of growing up in a multicultural hub – a taste for drinking Indian Chai tea with a foamy pull.

A full moon under normal circumstances

there would be the usual spot for the moon to appear. I was still checking my memory about the date of *Yuan Xiao* while doubting my sighting of a crescent moon several nights ago.

Then, the loud shattering boom interrupted all my thoughts.

It was much louder and deeper than any of the frequent fireworks displays that I had heard during festivals celebrations along the Dnipro River. As someone who had experienced explosions before, including during my military service or while shooting live action sequences for movie productions, instinctively I knew this was different.

The acoustic effects of the sound waves reverberating through the atmosphere of an anti-air interception was alarmingly new.

Before that moment, I was as detached as anyone watching the news when it comes to war. We have a tendency to treat it as "they are fighting over there." But from that moment onward, it transcended into "they are trying to kill us over here." Unlike Alice walking into her mirror, the war came charging out through my looking glass.

With all my internal alarm bells screaming out the gravity of the situation, realising that every citizen's life was in danger, I reined in my impulses and turned to walk back into the bedroom to tell my wife Natalia that I thought Kyiv has come under attack. She gave me a side glance before saying that I was just imagining things and tucked herself back under the blanket.

It was pointless to panic and too sobering to scream, so I could only return to the balcony to finish my *teh tarik* which had begun to get cold. My instincts were yelling for me to prep for war while my rational self was explaining that I needed to witness more than just a flash in the sky before crying up the whole town.

So I finished my *teh tarik* and continued to watch the uneventful flow of the Dnipro River as the night remained as silent as usual. Sub-consciously not wishing for an attack on Kyiv, I showered and turned in for the night.

Then in the wee hours of the morning, a rapid succession of loud explosions was heard.

Hell had broken loose.

Starting with Many Bangs

BY THE TIME the sun rose, the influx of new messages had already surpassed our ability to read the earlier ones. The constant barrage of incoming information inundated us from every available media source, further fuelling our overflowing anxiety.

My thumb was shaking uncontrollably either from the non-stop scrolling of messages or surge of adrenaline from the accelerated heart beats, or both.

The possibility that Kyiv might fall had materialised into a reality.

Every airport around Kyiv has been struck by missiles, the invading Russians had opened up three fronts with attacks in the north, east and south of Ukraine, with their elite airborne units attempting a decapitation strike on the capital.

It made me wonder how people coped with panic attacks during the Second World War when all they had were short-wave radios and newspapers. In those days, being panic-stricken during such do or die situations really meant do or die.

Looking from our balcony I could see some of our neighbours quickly stuffing as many bags as possible into their cars which were parked by the side of the road with their engines running.

We scanned the news trying to understand the scale of attack being waged on the city of Kyiv. I knew the distance from Kyiv to the Belarus border was over a hundred kilometres. As long as there were no reported sightings of Russian troops around the north of Kyiv, we would have time to re-examine our plans before executing them. So we focused on collecting and prioritising information from areas north of Kyiv such as Chernihiv, Chornobyl, Ivankiv, Kozelets, Borodyanka and Vyshhorod in case of any amphibious assault.

Assuming that the Russian troops were mostly mechanized, they could cover the distance within a day if unchallenged. If challenged, it would give us more time to plan and manoeuvre.

If they remain unchallenged, I wondered how ready the citizens of the city were to face them.

President Zelensky of Ukraine had already declared martial law. All men between the ages of 18 and 60 were banned from leaving the country. A curfew would be imposed at 22:00 hours that night. All non-official traffic would be ordered off the roads. The call to take up arms and defend the country had already been issued. Ukrainians with military experience were requested to join the army or form militia groups.

There was an open invitation for foreigners with combat experience to join the foreign legion of the Ukrainian army. I have to confess that during moments like these, it required efforts to leash my temptation of answering the call to the wild.

We knew that contrary to what many people expected, President Zelensky did not flee. This meant that we had to ask ourselves if we were in the invaders line of attack for their decapitation strike on Ukraine. I quickly scanned my surrounding area on Google Maps to identify potential choke points for fighting and made mental notes of those locations in case of any breaches along the Northern or Eastern fronts. Looking at the possibility of aerial attacks, I was then no longer envious of my neighbours on the top floor with their airy roof terraces and sky gardens.

After establishing the pecking order in terms of anxiety for all incoming news, we decided our first task was to contact our immediate family before having breakfast.

While I beat the eggs for an omelette, my mind was busy filtering as much information as possible. Perhaps it was my experience with unexpected surprises while participating extreme sports, but I knew that accurate assessments were paramount. There are always a variety of options, each choices shrouded in doubt and accompanied by parameters beyond our ability to alter.

Since martial law had been declared, we hoped that there would still be law and order.

Weeks before the invasion, many embassies had been issuing warnings for their respective citizens to flee Ukraine by commercial means while it was still possible to do so. Back then I did a quick check online regarding the COVID travel restrictions into Singapore and realised that my wife Natalia together with our cats would not be able to get the vaccinations and documentation in time.

Catching an international flight during the COVID endemic was really challenging too. Many airport terminals had closed or were reduced to minimum operations, with the frequencies of flight routes getting scaled down or terminated. Booking these flights, paying the high costs and the hassle of quarantines made it impossible for us to make hasty arrangements.

At that time, the only country we could travel together without COVID restrictions was Egypt. We tried searching for apartments to rent along the coast of the Red Sea before the fighting broke out as it was a mecca for free diving.

However the moment those air strikes began over the capital, all airspace was closed by Ukraine with desperate calls to NATO to help with the enforcement of a no-fly zone. Our exodus was no longer an option. This meant that in order to maximise our odds of surviving the invasion, we had to break our limitations of ingenuity bounded by rationality during normal times.

We needed to stock up on food, water and necessities, which meant we needed cash. The day before, we had ordered three 40-litre barrels used for water dispensers in anticipation of any escalations. But that morning, the water delivery company announced that they were halting all operations because of the invasion.

So after breakfast we dressed up and we headed straight for our bank with empty backpacks. It was not that we had a lot of money but with the Ukrainian currency in free-fall of forty hyrinas to one US dollar, it would be more practical that we to use a large carrier for our cash, food and supplies. Besides if the attacks intensified, it would be easier to run with backpacks on our shoulders than with shopping bags in our hands.

We climbed down the flights of stairs, avoiding the lift in fear for being struck by a missile in mid-descent. Along the way, we passed another family engaging in nervous conversation with the security guard as we exited the safety of our apartment building.

With exposure to too many apocalyptic movies, we anticipated to meet with scenes of looting and robbery or to see civilization regress to the law of the jungle where the strong prey upon the weak. We had absolutely no idea how people were going to behave.

While there was palpable tension in the air, it did not feel like a lit fuse burning towards chaos. More like a boundless apprehension of solemness.

Approaching the bank from across the street, we noticed a long queue of people already waiting outside, the queue winded all the way around the block. As we debated whether it was worth our time to wait in line, a man emerged from the bank to announce that the branch had ran out of cash.

Without a car or available drivers on any ride hailing apps because making money had become less important than running for one's life, we concluded that it would not be an effective use of time for us to walk to the main branch and wait in another line for the chance to withdraw cash.

In war, our concept of time morphs differently, it was no longer about hours, minutes, appointments or schedules. All we cared about was when the current attack will stop and how long that pause going to last.

Natalia said that there was still money inside the petty cash drawer at the clinic where she was practicing traditional

Chinese medicine. We could use that to buy food and supplies since the clinic would not be operating for the time being. So we headed towards her clinic, which was a 30-minute walk away.

As we strained our thumbs scrolling through endless pages of information while walking towards the clinic, a sight caught my eye which was quite remarkable to say the least. In the midst of everyone trying to navigate their way out of the dire situation, I noticed an elderly lady in a yellow headscarf bending over with a poop bag.

She was walking her beagle.

The first thought that came to me was, "Is she out of her mind?"

The Russians troops had entered Kyiv and missiles were falling over our heads. The city might be in shambles, with food, water, electricity and communications facing jeopardy, and she was walking her dog.

But the very moment I completed that thought, it dawned upon me that she might be thinking that we were the ones who were out of our minds and overreacting. Spanning from under-reacting to overreaction was the vastness of normalcy during times of war.

Stocking Up

WE MANAGED TO enter the compound where the clinic was situated without incident, but the rows of shops were eerily quiet, a stark contrast to their usual bustle on a normal weekday morning. Considering that none of the full glass panel units had been smashed or broken, orderly behaviour was still prevailing in this neighbourhood.

Natalia found another stash of cash that she had kept to pay the upcoming rent. It was an unexpected discovery, like finding a lottery ticket with a small winnings stashed among dirty laundry. We were grateful for the clause in the lease agreement that allowed for termination under unforeseen circumstances. We were hoping that an unprovoked invasion by Russia would qualify as one.

While we were in the clinic, it dawned on me that we should also be stocking up on medical supplies in addition to food and water. However, as that was a TCM clinic, our options were limited to disinfectants and bandages. As we scoured the clinic for supplies to scavenge, we stumbled upon the water dispenser and next to it stood an unopened 40-litre barrel of drinking water.

When we received the call from the water delivery company cancelling all deliveries in the morning, we were quite worried about the reliability of our water supply in an urban environment. Because situated upstream along Dnipro River was the Chernobyl power station which had reported sightings of Russian troops. Should that supply be contaminated radioactively, every city downstream will be direly affected.

Small reliefs, like finding a stash of cash or a barrel of water, go a long way in times of anxiety. We drank what was left inside the water dispenser before leaving with the new barrel.

I pride myself for exercising regularly and being decently fit, but while handling the barrel of water, I developed a newfound respect for the water delivery men. While they may have used trolleys for most of the work, in an old European city like Kyiv, there are still plenty of walk-up apartment buildings.

It reminded me of the cooking gas delivery men I used to see in the seventies who always came by with a towel draped over their shoulder. Now I finally understood that the towel was not for wiping sweat from their laborious work but for traction to prevent the round gas canisters from rolling or sliding off their shoulders with every step.

As February was still cold, the winter jacket I was wearing was wind proof and rather slippery. So I decided to improvise and draped Natalia's scarf over my shoulder to get better control carrying the water barrel. Together, we made our way back to our apartment.

After walking two thirds of the way, we reached a cross junction. Straight ahead was our apartment, while turning left would lead us to the supermarket. Natalia suggested that she head to the supermarket to grab as many things as possible while I return to our apartment with the water before meeting her back in the supermarket later on.

Although I had performed many of similar parting scenes throughout my acting career, I had never experienced such an overwhelming flood of emotions when such a scene came true to life. We hugged and kissed each other tightly, knowing that it was a necessary decision and parted with the unspoken fact that we were taking separate paths after the rockets have rained.

As I made my way back to our apartment, I quickened my pace by trotting as fast as I could without letting the water barrel fall off my shoulder. I tried to steady my breathing while passing others who were also weighed down and struggling with overloaded shopping bags.

But the time I finally arrived at the lobby of our apartment, my shoulders were starting to ache from all that weight and the distance I had covered. As I stared up the stairwell and contemplated the option of taking the lift, I knew the pace that I could climb those stairs would not match my desire to be reunited with Natalia but neither would I want to risk taking the lift in event of a missile strike.

In the end, I placed the water in the lift and sent it up to our floor, while I ran up the stairs myself. Fortunately, I managed to reach our floor seconds after the water's arrival as it really was not the time nor place to be playing cat and mouse with a barrel of water.

I opened the door to our apartment and placed the barrel onto the floor with a heavy thud. I hurriedly emptied my backpack by dumping its contents into a messy pile in the foyer. As I looked up, I saw our cats Tiger, Misha, Aristocat and Bolshevik staring at me nervously. Some people claim that cats have an intuitive sense and have the uncanny ability to pre-empt when something is about to happen. It certainly felt true in that moment.

I made my way to the supermarket with great haste. After passing through the automatic doors, I met another astonishing sight. Every available cashier counter was in operation and long queues of people stretched down the shopping aisles, spanning the entire depth of the supermarket.

The atmosphere was frantic as everyone scrambled to buy cartful of supplies while cashiers worked at lighting speed to scan the items as fast as they humanly could. It felt like the house was on fire with every man for himself but no one was yelling.

Every incorrectly pasted label, fruits that were not weighed or suspended credit card transaction was met with firm assurance and solved quickly by the staff on steroids. The staff in the supermarket were in battle mode, suppressing their own set of worries and anxieties by showing up to work during the onslaught of an invasion, hauling crates of supplies on pallet jacks from their storage, while shoppers left with bags near bursting point. This devotion of the supermarket staff to their work gave shoppers the reassurance they needed, and had helped to keep panic buying in check.

I hoped the invaders had not crippled Ukraine's communications systems and that the cellular networks would still be working when I tried to call Natalia on her phone. To my relief, she responded with a photo of herself queuing somewhere between rows of toothpastes and detergents. Seeing her standing in line with other doomsday shoppers while clutching a large bag of cat litter was quite comical.

IX SHEN

Top: Rows and rows of empty shelves as shops and businesses started to close in preparation for war.

Left: Rows of nervous shoppers taming their panic

Because the number of people rushing to do their doomsday shopping was so overwhelming, every shopping cart had been snatched up. Natalia had only managed to grab a shopping cart meant for children. Even so, she had stuffed buckwheat, cabbage and cat food inside the tiny but colourful shopping cart while a bunch of bananas hung flimsily over the advertisement flag for some brand of candy which I do not remember.

I opened my backpack and stuffed whatever else that she had been shuffling along on the floor into the bag and told her to wait for me in the queue while I scavenged for more supplies.

Using the food pyramid as a guide, I began my hunt for carbohydrates and squeezed towards the grains section hoping to find some rice. I came across some pricey imported Basmati rice. Not our usual purchase but during wartime, it will do. Displayed on another shelf were bulgur, so I took two one-kilogram bags and left.

Heading to where the flours were on display, I found two packets of flour still sitting on the entire row. They were left on the shelf because both had damaged packaging and were spilling flour out. I chose the one that spilled the least and made my way through the horde towards the fruits section planning to use those plastic bags meant for weighing to contain the bag of spilling flour.

While placing the packet of flour into a bag, I decided to grab some pears as well. As winter was drawing to an end, the variety of fruits became ever more limited. Those mandarins that were still on the shelf appeared to be quite smashed. Thankfully, we still had a decent amount of fresh fruits at home. But if fresh deliveries were to become unpredictable, we would be at risk of scurvy for no one can predict how long the fighting will last. Some broccoli and Chinese cabbage were also available at the fresh produce section, so I just added them to our fibre food group.

The butchery was a complete disappointment. What was usually filled with a large variety of different cuts of meats had become an empty display. I glanced at the dehydrator, where there were still two slabs of dry-aged beef but decided against paying for protein at those prices.

The crowded seafood counter was left with a very limited selection which I knew would probably be sold out by the time I am served by the fishmonger.

I skipped the frozen section because we had filled our freezer to the brim last week in preparation for a scenario like this. At that moment, we were proud of our decision, but it was also a situation we would rather be wrong about.

Our remaining choices for protein were the preserved ones. I stuffed two large sausages from an unfamiliar brand and a block of cheese from the chilled section into my backpack which had grown rather heavy by then.

Ukrainians have a rich tradition with sausages and dairy products. I suspected the reasons that they are still decently stocked were because – A, the supermarket staff had been restocking almost as fast as they were being sold. B, most homes would still be stuffed with them from the festivities. C, the tastiest ones are usually handmade, so mass productions from the factories are usually shunned except in times of war.

After shutting the glass door of the sausage chiller, I noticed another stand alone chiller nearby. Inside were stacks of colourful boxes of packaged tofu almost completely untouched. Tofu is still a novelty item in Europe and sold in exotic packaging. It was a far cry from my memories of the wet market seller cutting up slabs from a large block of Tofu on a wooden tray. Knowing how Tofu helped win many wars in Asia, I took about a third of the entire stock, especially since they were discounted.

As I walked back to Natalia, I passed shelves of canned fishes. To my surprise, not many people were buying them. I come from a time when the military rations consisted only of canned food and we did not have the luxury of tri-laminated retort pouches back then. Seeing rows of canned food was quite unbelievable considering the situation we were facing. That was when I realised that not everyone was buying rationally.

Grateful for my repertoire of tofu recipes

A man was filling his trolley with cookies and biscuits, while a lady had her arms fully stretched out, struggling to hold a large stack of frozen dinners, and a group of elderly gentlemen were busy discussing which vodkas were on discount. Still feeling a little surreal, I grabbed a whole carton of canned sardines and went in search of Natalia who had only moved less than twenty metres since I left.

Everyone was buying with trolleys that were filled to maximum capacity and I could only assume that from the previous experiences during the initial lock down periods of COVID, shoppers must have rehearsed for this panic buying.

Because everyone was buying in preparation for the end of the world, seemingly unpanicked, though incubating the thought of being struck by a missile while standing in a treacherous check-out line.

As we inched towards the cashier, we tried to estimate how much our grocery bill would be since we only had a limited amount of cash on us. Despite the hive of the non-stop barcode scanning, I could still hear the familiar beeps of credit card payments, which had a rather distinct tone.

I shared with Natalia the possibility of electronic transactions since the supermarket lights are still on and our phones were showing cellular coverage. Without hesitating, she shouted the question at the cashier about five metres away. The cashier replied loudly that electronic transactions were possible but only for cards issued by two particular banks.

That information rippled down the queues with a domino effect as everyone disseminated the information like a bushfire, every shopper silently understood our common worry – chaos might reign should the payment system collapse.

While Natalia was relieved to have a card from one of the issuing banks, I marvelled at the camaraderie among the people. No one was delusional about our current situation but the civility and cooperation I witnessed were the Ukrainian version of 'Kampong spirit'.

Locating True North

WE RETRIEVED OUR backpacks filled with groceries from the lift after climbing the stairs to our apartment. Safe in the quiet of our home, isolated from the hyped-up crowds, our imagination began to run wild with all kinds of worst-case scenarios as the battle raged on. Natalia and I were discussing a multitude of options for our next course of action while we put away supplies in our kitchen cabinets.

It wasn't until our cats interrupted, reminding us that it was past their lunchtime that we realised how much our thinking had been influenced by adrenaline.

During stressful life and death situations, the act of trying to find the most logical choice out of all available choices is quite an illogical act itself, driven primary by one's desire to survive. Not wishing to be in a prolonged state of poor mental health by allowing the amygdala to lead the frontal lobe, we turned our focus towards the cats.

We were thankful for the simple chore of preparing a cats' meal to recalibrate our thoughts. There is a saying in Mandarin which describes the state of disorientation we felt then – 找不着北 or being unable to find one's true north. We appreciated the solace of watching our cats gobble up their food when we heard urgent knocking on our door.

Our neighbour Elena was checking in on us to see if everything was alright. No stranger to invasions, she had evacuated from the disputed region of Pridnestrovia in Moldova during the Russian-backed Transnistria War in 1992 and moved to Ukraine. Elena invited us over for tea at her home, so we could discuss everything with calmer minds, we agreed eagerly since we had no appetite for lunch ourselves.

We gathered around my Chinese tea set over a pot of green tangerine Pu-erh tea to exchange information. Elena's daughter joined us while her husband and son-in-law went to the local registry to update their personal information with the registry which all Ukrainian men had to do.

Everyone threw everything into the discussion by regurgitating whatever information we had. Putting our minds together, we dissected and digested the developing situation in hopes of making sense out of it all.

We concluded that as much truth there is in hype, it can be needlessly misleading because every belligerent has its own information and disinformation campaigns. While the news agencies and media were serving their own needs and viewership ratings. The plethora of perspectives on our common situation therefore yielded a spectrum of varying narratives.

We realised that it was important to prioritise information by dividing into categories of 'dangerous', 'danger close' and 'danger far'. We would focus on our immediate neighbourhood if any hostile forces popped up into view, followed by a 20-kilometre radius of the transportation network and

50-kilometre radius of invaders amassing in threatening numbers.

As for air strikes, that came down to the question of staying or leaving the city. With increasing reports of petrol stations closures, we understood that strategic assets such as fuel might become unavailable during times of war. Elena also shared her experiences of evacuating from Moldova twenty years ago, where people had gotten robbed due to the type of cars they were driving as law and order deteriorated.

With the war dynamically evolving, we could not identify an evacuation plan with well-planned routes, sufficient refuelling and rest stops to any destination of relative safety. Staying put was thus the better option at that moment.

Although opening up the weapon armoury for citizens to take up arms and make Molotov cocktails were good for morale, it was not really effective in military sense. We knew from the Chechnya and Syrian wars that the Russians only entered the cities after demolishing them. So the odds of dying from hunger and thirst might be higher than the risk of firing a rifle or tossing a Molotov bottle.

Despite the intelligence provided by Western and Russian agencies, no one on the ground believed that the invaders would be able to just stroll into Kyiv and govern. Prior to the invasion, the Ukrainians I met were adamant with a common belief that armed Russians would not be welcome. Russia's sudden invasion despite officially proclaiming that they had no intentions a week ago only reiterated the Ukrainians' belief.

During Ukraine's darkest hours, President Zelensky's decision not to leave the capital in times of need permitted everyone to rally behind one leader. Everyone had faith that the Russians' advance would be met with resistance while praying that Kyiv would not fall. Although the proverbial elephant had been quietly sitting in the room, nobody wanted to discuss the potential for nuclear escalation.

    Having decided to stay, our next course of action in terms of priorities – safety, food, water, power and communications. With safety as our main agenda, we began to identify high risk areas within and around our apartment building.

Surviving vs Planning

OUR CATS WERE already taking their naps by the time we returned to our apartment. Seeing how carefree they were while lazing in their hammocks make us envious. It took a while for me to realise that they should not be lazing those hammocks. Because they were windows mounted. Windows with a view may add value to a property but they also triple the safety risks in times of war.

Not only it would have a spectacular view of any nearby explosions, the windows would not stop anyone from experiencing the shockwave as well. It is recommended to stay behind at least two layers of load bearing walls during an attack. So subtracting our exterior wall, we discovered

Aristocat enjoying his view on the hammock

that only our guest toilet or the walk in wardrobe met the recommendations.

We decided against sleeping in the fire escape stairwell as the remaining neighbours in our apartment building might be using it for evacuation and the stairwell was a poorly ventilated smoke free passage as well. Ideally a bomb shelter should be constructed underground, the deeper it goes, the safer it is. Until military scientists invented those bunker busters – which made bunkers become death traps as well.

Most buildings constructed during the Soviet era had underground bunkers while pre-Soviet buildings from the Tsarist dynasty had walls more than a meter thick. Back then the industry's reputation took precedence over cost cutting capabilities and those architectural structures were solidly built. They might look eerily Gothic during twilight hours but they do generate an awkward sense of security while you are inside, especially when the outside environment appears to be even more threatening.

Our underground solution was the carpark in our basement which was not very deep but underground none the less. We paid a visit to the resting quarters of our building security team which was inside the carpark and received updates about the latest developments. Half of the residents' parking lots were emptied as most of the foreigners living in our building had fled the country. We were advised to keep all windows and doors bolted and shut, as the risk of saboteurs or looters were very real.

We scoured the carpark looking for sites where we could take cover during air raids. In the end it was a coin toss between one far end corner where there was a power socket near an exit or in between the columns around the lift shafts. Jokingly, we concluded that the only way to decide was to try both venues in an event of an air raid. Though in truth, by the time we hear missiles exploding over our heads, it too may be a coin toss on whether if we could make it down to our carpark in time.

On the first day of the invasion, there was a constant barrage of information coming in. Official warnings were rapidly replaced by a tsunami of other personal messages due to the default design of our smart phone notifications. Reflecting on the documentary "The Social Dilemma", this notification function on our phones can both save and kill us. It saves us by delivering the vital information and kills us by obscuring the vital information among the unimportant ones.

We spent a considerable amount of time scrolling through all the different messaging and social apps to identify the official and credible accounts in order to pin their messages on the top as means to filter out speculative sources.

It made me realise that our grandparents generation could skip this information filtration process during the Second World War, for back then, there were only short-wave radios, newspapers and the town crier. During our information age, we like to pride ourselves as having the ability to plan ahead. But when the excrement hit the fan, our survival instincts just kicks in by scattering many theories out the window.

As the sun began to set and evening approached, I instinctively switched on the lights to prepare for dinner. Natalia turned them off in horror.

That was when I realised that light discipline had slipped my mind. You would not want to stand out by being the only lit up unit in a dark building along a blackout neighbourhood. A curfew had been imposed across the country – our windows were to be bolted, curtains undrawn and illumination kept to the minimum.

I took out my trail running headlamp but discovered that the red-coloured illumination made it near impossible to figure out when the meal was cooked in the frying pan. Everything is uniform in colour or until things begin to carbonize. I made a mental note to stick to the electric cooker when preparing meals in the dark.

Gone Bumping in the Night

DURING A MILITARY invasion, a bedroom with a view only creates nightmares without the need to fall asleep. We decided to designate our walk-in wardrobe as our main resting area and went about preparing it for night.

First, we had to transfer out many stuff lying about inside the wardrobe. We stacked them into the bedroom which was fast resembling a storeroom. As the wardrobe was located in an unheated section within the apartment, we piled additional blankets on the floor in case Kyiv loses its capacity to provide heating.

We unrolled the yoga mats to serve as cushioning and brought in our coffee table to place our laptops. With no windows, we allowed ourselves the illumination of a small table lamp so we did not have to live in darkness. Our cats were curious about why we were crowding into the walk-in wardrobe and decided to join the pyjamas party.

At that moment, we realised that we might have difficulties evacuating with them to our basement should there be an air raid. So I decided to install a turn-out equipping station. Anyone who has served in an active military unit will understand that there are different level of readiness. These levels are usually coded into colours like yellow, orange and red.

Red meant that we were loaded and ready to roll, while yellow would be relatively relaxing, lying in our bunk beds staring at the ceiling fans. But with all gears well laid out and organised at the turn-out equipping station ready for equipping at a moment's notice.

We needed to set this up next to our main door in the foyer.

I took another backpack and started packing things that we needed to survive an air raid. I hoped that my estimation of a twelve-hour raid would be the maximum sustainable duration for the current campaign, not due to any military intelligences but because daybreak would introduce a different rhythm. It was just a guess.

The contents of the backpack included water, dried rations, power banks, cat food, snacks, sleeping bags, matches, a camping stove and books for reading. As for our personal attire, we had prepared helmets, goggles, ear plugs, gloves, elbow and knee pads, torches, masks and walkie talkies. All neatly arranged and prepped to grab on the fly.

We decided it would be more practical to place two cats into each carrier in case we need to run, as it is easier to run down the stairs holding one carrier with two hands rather than risking losing our balance and stumble down the stairs juggling a carrier on each arm. Each cat weighs about five kilograms and I knew how difficult it would be to cross the traffic lights junction in a hurry with one cat per carrier in each hand, so we lined the carriers with our cats' favourite blankets and placed them next to the turn-out station.

IMPRESSIONS OF AN INVASION

Since winter sports are our regular activities, we thought it would be most practical to sleep in our thermal underclothes if we needed to suit up and flee. We would likely freeze in our pyjamas if we had to hole up in the basement the whole night.

While we were discussing toilets options for the cats, explosions started to resonate like thunder without a storm. Our survival instincts just kicked in, scattering the cats into different hiding corners around the whole apartment. So much for theories and planning.

Natalia immediately went to search for them.

I changed into my alpine attire and put on my protection gear while Natalia tried to catch Tiger who was hiding behind the headboard in our bedroom. I told her to leave the cats alone, we had to protect ourselves first, just like putting on emergency oxygen masks on an airplane.

Natalia handed Tiger to me and started to put on her alpine attire. I placed the cat into a carrier and took out a pack of their favourite snacks and started shaking it vigorously. A trick I learnt from of filming with animals.

I closed the doors of each room as they bounded out for their snack, I wanted to keep them within the foyer because it was nearly impossible to find a hiding cat in a dimly lit environment while explosions rattled the sky. Once we had all the cats securely placed into the carriers, we rewarded them with snacks.

I slung the backpack over my shoulder and exited our apartment. The abrupt brightness of the lighting inside the stairwell was blinding because our eyes were accustomed to the dim environment at home. As we descended the levels, we could hear our neighbours above entering the stairwell with their kids in tow as everyone was rushing toward the basement as quickly as possible.

When we arrived at the basement carpark, some of our neighbours had already gathered. Everyone greeted each other with friendly but worried nods. It was an unfortunate circumstance for a block party.

We decided to settle ourselves near the exit area as it was cleaner than the space in-between the lift columns. I found some empty cardboard cartons and placed them on the cement floor. The cats were nervous but cosy when we placed their carriers next to each other.

Hoping to check for new information, I took out my phone but there was no data service available. Only old school voice calls or messages. I sat with the cats while Natalia mingled with the neighbours for updates.

Everyone was trying to handle the situation as calmly as they could. A few elderly ones started a game of backgammon on a disused cardboard carton, while a couple walked their dog in a closed loop within the carpark. The teenagers were busy testing their network signals at various corners while others tried to get some sleep inside their cars.

Most of us were bomb bunker first timers.

Everyone understood that this was an unwanted situation and getting anxious or emotional would not change anything. As the explosions went off around the city, it seemed to me that dignity and hysterics might have been inversely proportional.

Perhaps due to the proximity to the exit, a constant flow of cold air numbed my legs. I got up and joined our neighbourhood chat group. Many were surprised that I was still in the country as many foreigners had already left.

Despite the lack of cellular network signals, information was still available. The television set inside the security guards quarters of our building broadcast state news, while our neighbours called a wide network of relatives and friends; the teenagers spread any updates they received while they shuttled up and down the stairwell posting new videos of themselves.

We returned to our awaiting cats and sat down on flatten cartons. Although they were warm and cosy together, the exterior of their carriers felt chilly due to the flow of the cold air. We decided to relocate to the space in-between the lift columns in case we had to spend the entire night inside the underground carpark.

I borrowed a broom from the security guard quarters and began to tidy up the space we spotted earlier. By the time we had moved everything and made ourselves as comfortable as we could in our new site, the security guard announced that the air raid alert had ended. However we were advised to remain underground as the probability of more air strikes was going to be high before daybreak.

Most of the neighbours made a beeline for the carpark exit but we decided to wait until the crowd cleared. We were already decently settled in our little corner and it would be a pity not to relish the fruits of our labour. I took off my helmet and leaned against the wall to rest my back, checking my watch. It was already past two in the morning.

Realising that we had been mentally wound up for the last twenty odd hours since the explosions had woken us at five in the morning the day before, I couldn't help but think about how our flight or fight responses during life and death situations make insomniacs out of us. I am no stranger to adrenaline surges from my extreme sports adventures, but this felt like an overdose.

As I pondered how to obtain information if the phone networks came under attack, Natalia abruptly fell asleep next to me. Even though the carpark had emptied out, I decided it would be better for us to catch some sleep on the carpark floor than to reverse the whole process of getting back to our apartment.

Using my helmet as an eye shade, I tried to catch some shut-eye. Our cats, however, had other plans. The silence of the carpark seemed to make them even more restless and fidgety. And they prevented us from getting any decent rest. Perhaps they are more attuned to their sense of security than humans.

I got up and took a stroll round the carpark. I realised that except for the security guards, we were the only ones still sheltering in the cold basement. When I returned, Natalia was awake thanks to the cats.

We had to decide whether to stay put until daybreak, which was only a few hours away or return to our apartment so the cats could be freed from their carriers. I was not worried about them because they had previously flown in their pet carriers for over thirty hours inside airplanes cargo holds. Except then, there was no one they could emotionally blackmail to free them by coaxing the person with their whines of displeasure.

In the end we decided to haul them up the stairs because it was impossible to get any decent rest with their non-stop meowing. The alternative would be to let them out from the carriers to go about exploring the carpark, but we did not want the drama of showering four cats as the last 24 hours had been dramatic enough.

In the end, our decision paid off as there were no more air raids during the wee hours of the morning. Natalia and I were instantly knocked out on our yoga mats the moment we arrived back into our apartment.

Strength from Survival

IT WAS NEARLY noon when we woke up the next day. We only managed to catch a couple hours of sleep after switching our phones into silent mode to avoid the constant alerts which induced an unhealthy amount of non-essential anxiety.

When I sat up on the floor of our walk-in wardrobe and stared at the mirror, the awakening process of yawning and stretching felt almost like waking up any other day even though we were under extremely different circumstances from our normal routine.

I was intrigue by our attitude towards the surrealism of our reality. The city had been attacked and we were still alive.

Anyone who has experienced a sparring session would be able to relate that it is not the pain or shock that startles you when you get hit in the face. It is that smell which was both familiar and alien at the same time. As corny as it might sound, what doesn't kill you does make you stronger. We contacted our immediate families and close friends to update them before screening through the barrage of information.

Russian forces were reportedly about 30 kilometres north of Kyiv while the Chernobyl Nuclear power plant had been captured. The flood of updated images on social media was an unexpected phenomenon. During the US-Vietnam conflict, the news crew had almost free access and no censorship, despite the amount of time and distance it took for film stock to be ready for the distribution, so I knew how media can impact the war narrative, especially so for the invading forces.

The fact that our wifi and 4G were still functioning baffled me. Later, I found out that the cyber warfront had already begun before the Russian tanks started rolling. I had to credit the Ukrainians for their capability over technological warfare, for the communication networks were still functioning despite the unrelenting attacks. Seizing the opportunity, Ukraine made all cellular communications free of charge and any SIM card became usable across all network providers.

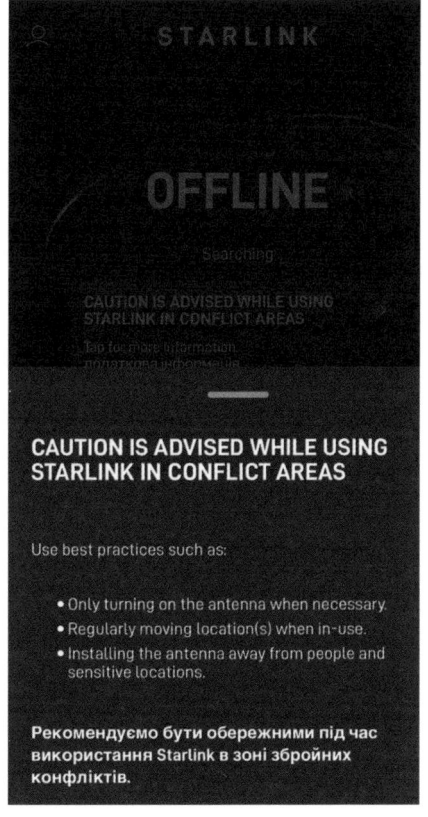

And just like that, the Russian invaders found themselves enveloped in a local labyrinth of hostile intelligences. Providing up to date information complete with GPS data. Not every civilian might had taken up arms, but they definitely all had smartphones. The informational war was just as intense as the physical one.

IX SHEN

The sound of approaching jets suddenly filled the air and it made us rush toward the balcony. Flying low and fast, two military jet fighters headed northwards along the Dnipro river. From their twin tail fins, I assumed they were MiG-29s. Although I was unable to identify whether they were friend or

The Dnipro River – a place where the Vikings rowed their boats, children fly their kites and jets approach their bombing runs.

foe, but since they came from the south, I guessed they could not have been too unfriendly.

As more and more Russian troops tried to approach the city, the sanity of a siege city began to stretch. Seeing war planes skimming over water surfaces along the same slots where children kites would normally fly, we did not panic but felt jubilant instead, because it meant that the Ukrainians were fighting back.

We saw notifications of the weapons armoury being opened up for citizens to withdraw assault rifles for those that met the registration requirements. Preference were given to those who had combat experience. Neighbourhoods militias were sprouting out everywhere with extra emphasis along the areas along the axis of approach towards the centre of Kyiv.

The citizens of Kyiv were risking their lives to protect their beloved city. Recipes for Molotov cocktails were shared around feverishly like a festive delicacy. Procedures for reporting on invaders information were being simplified and streamlined.

Verbal challenges were instructed to civilians, helping everyone to identify impostors and saboteurs. A simple phrase – strawberry, became a cultural password. The Ukrainian intonation of strawberry is distinctively different from the Russian, even if one could reproduce the vocalisation it would still be quite impossible to synchronise that particular intonation with corresponding emotion without a significant amount of Ukrainian cultural inflection. It was simple but remarkably innovative. Instinctively even children could distinguish whether this person was native or not. After all, nearly 80 percent of communications is non-verbal.

Whether governmental or private civilian groups, everyone rallied around and organised to contribute in any way possible. The people's resilience had turned into resolve.

Bonfire of the Placidity

NATALIA RECEIVED A call from her colleague living on the other side of Kyiv that the airport near her flat had been stuck by missiles and the water supply to their flat had stopped.

We knew that Ukrainians forces were fighting to take back Hostomel airport near the north western side of the city. The Russian elite airborne paratroopers managed to get a foothold of the airport. With Russia's enormous amount of airlifting capabilities, an airport less than 40 kilometres away from Kyiv was like a floodgate that was too unimaginable to be opened.

With the prospect of water shortages looming, I decided to convert our bathtub into a water tank while we still had running water. I began tying makeshift rope handle to carry of our 40-litre water barrel. While it was possible to carry the barrel over my shoulder when sealed, it would be a challenge to use it to fetch water. Although the Dnipro River was nearby, I should prepare for worst case scenario after reports of Chernobyl Nuclear plant upstream being occupied by the Russians. As a precaution, I decided to check the nearest artesian well, now that the curfew had been lifted.

There was some light traffic within the city, though the usual parked cars by the roadside were becoming a rare sight. It was reassuring to see a public bus stopping at the bus stop alighting passengers. I could not imagine what would be going through the bus driver's mind during an air raid, wouldn't he be forced to choose between speeding down the quiet roads or remaining stationary? With business closed and offices shut, peak hour traffic took on a whole new meaning.

I arrived at the artesian well and was relieved to find it operational. With the unpredictability of battle, I understood that having access to water supply was more urgent than food. Walking through the quiet neighbourhood might offer a sense of security but observing from a ground level in an urbanised environment was limiting my situational awareness uncomfortably. Taking the risk that there might not be any imminent air strike, I chose to detour by the river on my way back. February's sun might have thawed the midstream but there was still ice on the riverbanks, which meant I would have to bring along an axe to fetch water from the river.

A plume of smoke was rising on the opposite bank, which was odd since I did not hear any explosions. As I ventured closer, I saw an Ukrainian military truck parked next to a governmental looking building that did not appear to be damaged. Armed soldiers were securing the perimeter and feeding a bonfire by dumping documents into a steel drum. Likely a fallback protocol.

As brave and resilient the citizens of Kyiv might be, the impending doom of the advancing invaders was inducing everyone to seek for strength from within. Feeling grave, I headed back towards my apartment.

IMPRESSIONS OF AN INVASION

A historical city, these old Artesian wells supplied Kyiv with naturally filtered water before the modernisation of water utilities.

As surreal as it seemed, people were still waiting for the green lights before crossing a traffic junction. Bewilderingly, I stood at a traffic junction waiting for the little green men to appear, while hoping that a missile would not land where I was standing, because I think I will have a molecular rearrangement before I can finish saying "molecular rearrangement".

I could feel vibrations through my feet as a deep rumble echoed around the corner. Drawing from my experiences working on a film set with a company of tanks, I knew that mechanised vehicles always announced their arrival before showing up. But witnessing an Infantry Fighting Vehicle (IFV)

thundering past our neighbourhood bakery was a sight to behold as I could imagine the familiar rows of buns bouncing in unison behind those locked shutters.

The men in green appeared and disappeared quickly in the direction of the river. If it wasn't for the fluttering blue and yellow flag at the front of the vehicle, I would have peed in my pants and regretted not having jaywalked earlier because it would have meant crossing path with the invaders, or it might have been the ground vibrations caused by the proximity of the IFV which was too close for my bladder. I saw the steely determination on the vehicle commander's face and realised that the Ukrainian defence was not going to deteriorate like some foreign analysts had predicted. I continued to wait patiently for the little green men in the pedestrian lights to appear.

By then, the word of my presence in the capital of Ukraine had already gotten around to many of my friends, with a large chunk of them working in the media industry. Suddenly I found myself giving interviews one after another. Many viewers might have been shocked to witness my live interview being interrupted by an air raid alert but that was the fundamental reason for news to go live in the first place.

Live reporting is not merely about standing at an outdoor location, saying a prepared script into the camera, but to report the live events as they unfold while preparing for any unforeseen eventualities.

Opposite page:
The Temple of St. Nicholas – the patron saint for travellers of long journeys.

The most memorable for me was a radio interview for Channel NewsAsia 93.8FM. Unknown to most, interviewees like us had to dial in for audio and visual checks ten minutes before the scheduled broadcast time. After logging into the meeting room and while adjusting my audio level, I heard the first shot of a rifle. I assumed the studio team must have been at a loss when I suddenly ducked down and vanished from their screen. It was unlikely that the sound of the gunshot was loud enough for them to understand why I had disappeared. Maybe because the condenser microphone that I was wearing might had filtered out the rifle shot together with most of the background noise.

As the ensuing fire fight broke out, I tried my best to describe the situation while taking cover behind a wall without realising that the camera on my phone was facing an empty wall where I once stood. Despite it being a radio interview, I was not confident in articulating the unfolding scenario before me. I grabbed the leg of my tripod to bring the phone towards me.

The studio team must have realised it wasn't the ideal time to continue with the audio adjustments and decided to start recording immediately as I removed my phone from the holder. The IFV which I saw earlier was parked on the nearside of the bridge that spanned across the Dnipro river. This bridge was just a few hundred metres away from my apartment building and part of my usual jogging route. I had planned to conduct the interview near the fire escape of our building to show the wartime situation while remaining safely within of my apartment building.

IMPRESSIONS OF AN INVASION

Before the interview, I saw a black pick-up truck drive up to the bridge disembarking a group of men in civilian clothing, wearing bulletproof vests and carrying rifles that were not Kalashnikovs. Later, a three-tonner manoeuvred itself to park perpendicularly across the bridge forming a T-shaped roadblock adjacent to the IFV. Ukrainian troops in uniforms secured the bridge, diverting cars and pedestrians away from the area. Everyone was preparing themselves for the approaching Russians forces.

Danger close.

Enemy at the Gates

BY THE TIME the studio started to record the interview footage I had already been blabbering non-stop since taking cover behind the wall. I was trying to relay the information as quickly and accurately as the situation was unfolding before my eyes.

The Ukrainians had already taken up defensive positions on the near side of the bridge using whatever means of effective cover they could find, mostly staying behind vehicles, along the concrete parapets or lying flat on the tarmac.

The Russian advance had been so sudden that it was impossible to construct any form of fortifications. Those images of sandbags, hedgehogs and concrete slabs checkpoints in media news only started appearing a week later. So this was an old fashion you shoot me I shoot you type of gun battle.

By then I could differentiate between the shots, and most of the shots were from infantry rifles on the Ukrainian side, nothing automatic or heavy calibre.

I leaned outwards from the wall to get a better view and possibly to get a clearer understanding of the fire fight. That was when I spotted the black all-terrain vehicle (ATV) of the

Russian forces driving up the crest of the bridge, dressed in black tactical attire with goggles and masks covering their faces.

They seemed puzzled by the response they were receiving from the Ukrainians as their ATV began to slow down. They could not understand why the Ukrainians were fighting. My assumption of protocols for normal reconnaissance teams would be to disengage from any hostilities. But I saw the vehicle commander place his rifle on the side view mirror and begin to shoot.

I looked at the phone in my hand and decided that I couldn't possibly articulate everything that was unfolding before me. So I tried moving the phone camera over the banister to allow the studio to capture the action on the bridge while I ducked as low as possible.

That was when I heard the return volley of machine guns and heavy calibre weapons from the Ukrainians. Instinctively I knew it was too dangerous to stay and record the events, and that it would be safer for me to bolt to avoid the unnecessary risk of being hit by ricochets.

Without looking back, I retreated into the stairwell crouching as low as I could while the fire fight intensified. I later learnt that the visual portion of the fire fight had been edited out on YouTube due to its violent and graphic content. However, early viewers were able to see the uncensored version.

Back inside my apartment, I told Natalia about the fire fight on the bridge. It became clear to us that our windows, once a source of natural light and fresh air, were now a potential threat. We needed to reinforce them as soon as possible.

Without information about of the actual strength of the Russian forces on the bridge, I could not anticipate what the outcome would be. We could only imagine the worst. How would we cope if the city was overrun by the Russian forces? How would the Russians secure the environment? What counter offense the Ukrainians were going to take? Should we hide or surrender ourselves if there are house to house searches?

I knew the Presidential Palace was just up the hill after crossing the bridge, so any approach towards it would be fiercely contested. And once contested, it was impossible to predict the scale of escalation. So any passage leading into the heart of Kyiv may instantaneously turn into a battle front.

To use a metaphor, in the face of an avalanche surging down a mountain, you hope that the avalanche picks a path away from you or run out of momentum. The fire fight was intense but brief. The silence returned before my imagination had the chance to go into overdrive.

We dared not go near the windows and instead relied on our ears, scouring the internet for updates. We scrolled through the kaleidoscope of information on our phones, social media was awash with reports of civilian destruction by the Russian military as they advanced.

However, there were just as many private posts of civilians grabbing abandoned Russian military equipment as war trophies. The civilian resistance greeting the invaders was just as strong as the military one. Videos showed local teenagers planting the Ukrainian flag on top of 'Z' marked tanks, local hooligans disarming Russian soldiers and the now famous "gift of sunflower seeds" by an Ukrainian lady.

A few hours later, I heard the sound of a heavy vehicle stopping right in front of my apartment building. Unable to remain hiding in turtle mode any longer, I grabbed my monocular and walkie talkie before heading to the stairwell, telling Natalia to get the cats into their carriers and be ready for anything.

I returned to the spot where I had conducted the interview earlier. The was something smouldering on the far side of the bridge but my view was obscured by the crest of the bridge. The Ukrainian IFV was nowhere in sight, but a few soldiers in green uniforms were stationed on the bridge. I assumed they were Ukrainians.

I tried to look for the heavy vehicle below my apartment since I could hear its engine running, but my view was blocked. I entered the stairwell and descended two levels down the building. As I exited the stairwell, I heard the clack of boots walking below and sound of rifles clearing their chambers.

To my relief, I heard orders being shouted out in Ukrainian. I leaned over the banister and saw the exhausted Ukrainian soldiers sharing water and juices as they assembled themselves to board their heavy transport vehicle which had stopped in front my apartment. Judging from their uneven hair length, I surmised that these were reservists being called up for service at a short notice.

The area around my neighbourhood had been secured and the soldiers were being redeployed to fight elsewhere. Witnessing firsthand how the Ukrainians were defending their country, I was confident that the defenders would not disintegrate as many analysts had predicted.

Art Imitates Life

IT BAFFLES ME that many Russian soldiers genuinely believe that they were liberating a country oppressed by Nazis. Fact and fiction have become so intricately intertwined to the point that the very intent to distinguish between them can be exploited to pivot a war.

In this age of information, disinformation has become a potent weapon. History has demonstrated the immense influence of propaganda. On the other hand, we like to think that freedom of information could be our best defence against the emergence of another empire builder. But evolving equally on the other end of the spectrum were the specialists who spread disinformation as a tool to their advantage.

Why were the lives of ordinary citizens jeopardised? Why do technological advancements throughout civilisation continue to help those in power to end lives? And how did people from neighbouring nations end up battling to their death on bridges?

Without being overly philosophical about it, we understand that social animals wage wars. From well documented apes in the African jungles to the otters in the rivers of Singapore, nature has shown that there is an evolutionary reason for fighting. Whether it is a conflict for territory or battle for survival, territory and survival are interdependent and

Inextricably linked. Humankind seems to have reached a territorial agreement so everyone survives, or at least until that narrative is no longer agreeable.

I climbed back up the stairs excitedly relaying what I saw to Natalia over the walkie talkie. As I entered the apartment, our cats were ignoring me while exiting their carriers, they were probably rolling their eyes if they could.

All that anxiety and tension had taken a toll on everyone, and I needed to refocus on routine to recalibrate my state of mind. From the time the Russian troops crossed the borders until they showed up in our neighbourhood, it had been a fight or flight roller coaster ride for our mental states. Witnessing how the invaders could be stopped by Ukrainian determination, I reminded myself to just focus on breathing deeply.

The removal of cat litter had become a welcome mundane chore, though from the pungency of their urine we could tell that their adrenaline levels had been increasing too. We began to prepare dinner before sky grew dark as it was easier to oversee the cooking process. Constantly adjusting our activities to cope with the changes in our daily situations had become second nature to us, I could not differentiate if we were being adaptive or simply trying to survive.

While dining over a candlelight dinner might be romantic under most circumstances, we were not looking forward to using our candles. Because that would mean the electricity had been cut off. Besides, I discovered that the flickering flame of a candle does not help to calm nerves under duress.

So shortly after dinner, we agreed that we needed to take a break from all that outpouring of war time information. But our usual evening stroll had become an unsafe activity in times like these. We had to find something else that would not remind us about the war, like watching something entertaining online.

Since the Kremlin announced the recognition of the independence of the two eastern regions on 21st February, we had lost the mood for online entertainment as we understood that military escalation was imminent.

Logging into my Netflix account, I was aghast to see what was on my viewing list. There is much to reflect on oneself based on the type of content we choose to watch. In my profession, I specialise in the conceptualisation and execution of action sequences for movie productions.

For any action movie to sell, every action performance must be valued like a dialogue. If it did not serve the plot, it is excessive. So, by default, my viewing list included lots of content involving action, most of which inevitably involves battles or power struggles. The irony of watching them during times like this was too much to bear considering what we could see outside our windows.

Natalia's choice of binge worthy comedies was not appealing either. We were not in the mood for binging nor getting emotionally engaged with characters creating humour during peacetime melodramas. The challenge for us was finding content that could distract us from the atrocities of the ongoing invasion without sensationalising peacetime mediocrities. It was a coin toss between the Serbian film "On the Milky Road" or some forgettable documentary when we concluded that watching cartoons would be most ideal. Deciding between us which show to watch was never much of a fuss during normal times as there was always some other show or some other time for us to choose from. But when trying to maximise normalcy before the next air strike, the importance of the next available hour made it contentious. We literally needed an enchanted bubble to distract us from the reality and help us to survive the onslaught of negative thoughts.

Henceforth, we discovered the show "Disenchantment".

I am not sure whether it was the war scene between the Gnome and Org or the politically incorrect bickering of the ruling class. But the relatable absurdity against our surreal reality somehow had a calming effect as we entertained ourselves while waiting for the next air strike.

It could have been that the show was too entertaining or we had adapted to the sporadic fighting around Kyiv. Either way, we did not pay too much attention to our phones until the shock waves from an explosion rattled our windows.

By then I could already distinguish the explosions of aerial intercepts and I was sure that this did not sound like one. Which meant a missile or bomb of a sizeable warhead had impacted on the target and managed to detonate the entire destructive charge.

As I shook the packet of our cats' favourite snacks, I silently hoped that the Ukrainian air defence had not run out of interceptor missiles.

THE SECOND WEEK

Submerged trees in a village outside Kyiv – the plains where the Russian tanks had planned to cross were flooded by exploding the reservoir dam to save Kyiv.

Life Imitates Art

WHEN WE ARRIVED at the underground carpark, we noticed the number of people taking shelter had increased. After settling our cats into the corner, we walked around to get acquainted with the people hiding from the bombardment.

Some of them were not our neighbours living in the building. Several came from the outskirts where the Russian tanks were seen outside their homes. They managed to escape into the city centre to take shelter in the homes of family members or friends. Some were angry that they were forced to flee from their homes in prime residential districts, while others were either too distraught or relieved to be alive. But everyone was resigned to the fate that we were hiding underground like frightened animals.

We understood that there had been waves of airborne insertions by Russian troops around the outskirts of the city in conjunction with mechanised troops. Some had been repelled, but others were still fighting. A total of 17 battalion tactical groups have launched a combined attack on Kyiv. The area being highly contested was the Hostomel airport its surrounding areas.

There is an old Chinese military saying 三军未动，粮草先行, which is similar to the saying in English, "amateurs talk tactics, but professionals talk logistics." The invaders must have been out of their minds, or they were crazy enough to think that Kyiv would fall within three days.

One of the reasons why I was caught unprepared for the invasion, despite the large build-up of Russian forces during their openly declared military exercises along the borders of Ukraine, was that we had heard rumours about the lack of evidence for battlegroup-sized fuel convoys. We knew more or less the range and distance the invading force would have to fight to reach Kyiv. Without close logistical support, the forces fighting at the front wouldn't be able to sustain their push.

Comparatively, the close logistical support for 17 tactical groups would be so enormous that it would dwarf the military assets required for exercises. So their commander-in-chief had sent them deep into hostile territory, expecting them to take over the capital just by appearing.

Unbelievably, when the amount of people believing that the emperor is wearing new clothes reaches a critical mass, their belief becomes critical. Now I understood the puzzled look of the Russian soldier inside the ATV earlier in the day. We hoped that it would be only a matter of time before the invaders run out of steam or belief, and the Ukrainian defenders can counter-attack.

Most of the people were not prepared to spend the night in the cold underground carpark. They were anxious to return to their apartment units when the intensity of the rocket attacks became more intermittent and sparse. Hence, not all of us waited for the air raid alert to be called off.

We sat in the carpark as the people began to disperse and were faced with the choice of staying on the cold concrete floor or returning to the relative comfort of our walk-in wardrobe. Our cats were still snuggling together quietly inside their carriers, and I could not tell if it was because they were cold or felt it was safer to wait underground.

We thought that having access to updated information would help us decide. I went back up the stairwell in search of signal bars for new notifications. As I scrolled through the various updates of fighting around Kyiv, I noticed that there had not been any air strikes over our heads for a while. Calculating the risks, I climbed the stairs all the way up until I was a level beneath the rooftop and exited the stairwell.

The cityscape looked dystopic, both modern and primal at the same time. There was complete blackout. Although I could make out the outlines of the architecture against the faint illumination from the sky, the only visible details were the reflections off the glass windows and water surfaces. The silence was not eerie, just full of anticipation. It seemed like everything knew a storm was coming.

I scanned the horizon but did not see anything ablaze. Then through my peripheral vision, I caught a flash of two red lights. I turned in that direction but could not see anything except an enveloping dark mass. In doubt, I wondered if my imagination had been playing tricks on me when I saw a pair of brake lights lit up a little further away. I could make out a car driving down the road somewhere along the river harbour. I was curiously amazed by the driving skills of that driver who could operate a vehicle through the darkness without headlights or street lighting.

IMPRESSIONS OF AN INVASION

I immediately tensed up when I realised the driver must have been wearing night vision goggles. And the only reason one would drive with the headlights turned off is when the driver is aware that the enemy might be nearby. I subconsciously began to squat lower, starring at the dark mass in the general direction of the vehicle. It was quite a standard military procedure to attack twice as hard using the cover of darkness if a daytime attack had been repelled.

Recalling the fire fight earlier in the afternoon, I took out my phone to see if the camera's low light performance was as good as advertised. It was doubly disappointing as there is a distinction between low light and no light, and the flash illumination from my screen actually momentarily blinded my night vision. As I waited for the phosphenes of my phone screen to disappear from my retinas, I was totally dependent on my ears for situation awareness, that was when I heard a single shot being fired.

The shot did not sound like the weapon was firing away but towards my direction. I started to inch towards the entrance of my stairwell. For the next few minutes, there was just complete silence. Although my hand was gripping on the door handle of my stairwell, my feet were reluctant to move.

Was it a soldier testing his weapon? I tried running through my mind all possible scenarios to explain the single rifle shot. An anxious shooter who couldn't contain his nerves? Perhaps a sniper was taking out a target? All these questions were interrupted when a short burst of fire broke the suspense in the air.

From the sound, I could tell that it was located on the far side of harbour and facing away from me. Then a few rounds of return fire came from the opposite direction before I heard the full might of the ambush. It must have been a tsunami of bullets on the receiving end. It sounded like every available weapon was firing in full automatic mode, until their bullet magazines were emptied. I quickly stepped inside the stairwell when I heard a few ricochets bouncing off the roof of the building next to me.

Having participated in battalion-level live firing exercises before, I knew how challenging it was to synchronise everyone to fire at the same time. Whoever was commanding this ambush should be proud, as their firepower sounded like they were more than a battalion in size. It was a complete audio experience as I could not see any paths of tracer bullets at all.

The illumination inside the stairwell blinded me momentarily as I entered the well-lit environment out of the darkness. As the sounds of gunfire began to die down, I decided to head back underground since there was nothing to see.

I told Natalia that there was still fighting around the area, and it would not be very safe for us to return to our apartment. We felt reassured that the Ukrainians were fighting back valiantly and lifted our spirits by amusing ourselves with a TikTok video of Ukrainian gypsies joyriding on a stolen Russian tank. We decided that it would be more comforting to sleep in the carpark even though it wasn't as comfortable.

Setting into Motion

OUR CATS WERE most relieved when we finally got back into our apartment in the morning, and I mean this literally. All of them scooted to the litter boxes cramming together to relieve themselves. As for Natalia and I – we were starting to slide into a routine not meant to be normal.

Each daybreak meant that we had survived the night and there was a morning rush to reconnect with everyone. I now understood why birds in the wild chirp so feverish during daybreak. It was their way of rejoicing having not been eaten by predators that hunt during the night. Taking a cue from them, I realised that our nest needed to be reinforced as well.

The city imposed an extended curfew of 48 hours and I did not want to be suspected of espionage by being out in the streets, so I chose to spend the next two days on home improvements. Having bullets flying within earshot of one's abode would induce nervousness. And I prefer letting my nervousness spur some action. We could either indulge in our own fears, and continue sliding down a paralysis of paranoia, or accept the situation and keep improving our chances of survival.

I take back all my whining while carrying multiple bags of heavy kitty litter whenever we went shopping for cat supplies because we had quite a few bags in storage. Having some experience in trench digging, I knew that sandbags were good barriers against bullets. The finer the sand, the better they were. And our cats are really picky when it came to their toilets.

The idea was to absorb and scatter the kinetic energy of the bullet with minimum transference. I remembered this from my past when I performed butt party duties. Back then, we did not have a lot of electronic rifle shooting ranges and I noticed that the bullets could zip right through the wooden supporting frames but would splatter and pop on impact with sand. So I just needed our kitty litter to do the same for my windows.

With kitty litter padding the outside and sofa cushions the inside, I taped up the glass with duct tape to minimise any shards should the window panes shatter. What was previously a horizontal sofa for watching movies had become an additional vertical barrier against the windows. Even our bedframe and mattress were part of that barricade-themed interior décor.

I was pondering about the technical challenges of strengthening the curtain rails to support the weight of our carpet if I were to hang it when Natalia snapped when she stepped out from the shower.

It could have been the shock of our drastically changed interiors, fatigue from trying to survive the invasion, her suspicion that I was beginning to indulge myself with those home improvements, or all of the above. I was flabbergasted. I was trying to make our apartment as safe as I possibly

Right-side-up sofa when in vertical use

Park bridge – a popular jogging track along the Dnipro river

could since we decided not to leave and that was our first disagreement since the start of the invasion.

Staying harmonised in the midst of a military attack is something I consider to be the benchmark of a strong relationship. I heard of couples that ended up in bigger fights over smaller interior decoration decisions. So I understood that it wasn't the time nor place to continue any argument, and conceded by removing a few duct tapes from the mirror so she could blow dry her hair.

I continued to go around the building to inspect the fire-hoses and hydrants on the different levels. I was curious about the battleground around the neighbourhood but with the curfew still on, I had to wait till my next jogging session to find out – if that day ever came. When I returned to our apartment, Natalia's hair was dried and the mirror re-taped. We really had more pressing matters to attend to than to debate over the interiors. We looked like a pair of walking zombies dying for sleep.

Taking our mid-morning nap, we were suddenly awoken by loud banging at the door. It sounded harsh but not urgent. I needed to prepare myself mentally for anything that would transpire. I slipped on my shoes and checked the peep-hole warily. But I couldn't see anyone. So I cautiously opened the door and left it slightly ajar, peering from the sides. I was a little shocked when Daniel shouted my name.

Daniel is the two-year-old grandson of our neighbour next door, and that was why I couldn't see him through the peep-hole. He barged into our apartment because he wanted to play with our cats. His grandmother Elena came out from their apartment in hot pursuit. We sat down for a neighbourly gossip session about wartime over tea when that unavoidable sense of gloom began to set it.

We knew that the Russian forces had crossed more than a hundred kilometres from the border, their advances kept in check by the Ukrainians around the capital. The Irpin bridge was blown up and the village of Demydiv was flooded by water from the dam. But stopping the invaders advance was very different from driving them back because we knew that a big part for the stoppage was due to the over-stretched supply lines.

So, Kyiv's survival would be hanging in the balance as the invaders will be racing for fresh supplies, while Ukraine will have to muster troops from elsewhere to take on the supply lines while fighting their advance at the same time. No wonder they were mobilising so many men with military experience. Adding doom to the gloom was the latest satellite photographs of a Russian convoy – stretching over 20 kilometres in length – heading towards Kyiv.

Just as everyone was solemnly sipping their tea, Daniel suddenly broke out in giggles. He was delighted that our cat Misha was allowing itself to be hugged and kissed by him. Like an antidote for negativity, a child's laughter could uplift the gravity of the dire situation. We realised how much we desperately needed it.

Elena confessed that Daniel has been depressed for the last few days. Although he was unable to understand what was going on, he could sense that all the adults were feeling disturbed. It was not surprising that he came looking for our cats.

Natalia and I decided that we should organise a play session for all the children living in the building. Since the curfew had forbidden anyone to go outside, the only communal area that was safe for everyone would be the lift lobby on the ground floor. So we started a pets and children's' session during the evenings so that everyone could come together to hear the sound of laughter again.

Looking out for snipers while crossing the road

Sad and Sober

AFTER TWO CONSECUTIVE nights hiding in the bunker, as we climbed up the stairs towards our apartment in the morning after another interrupted night in the carpark, Elena greeted us at the corridor asking if we was ready to go to the supermarket. That was when it struck my fuzzy mind that the curfew would be ending soon.

If we did not get supplies, there was no telling when the next opportunity might arise. Releasing our cats from their carriers, I stuffed the IKEA shopping bags into my backpack and joined the shopping party gathering at the lift lobby. We might think that group buying was a peacetime activity to maximise discounts, but during wartime it was really more for safety in numbers.

When we exited our building into the cold morning, no one could say for sure what was going to happen. The senior members were recalling stories about civilians being targeted by snipers during the Euro Maidan in 2014 with the goal of causing panic and mistrust. Instead of walking on the sidewalk by the main road, we had to take a detour through alleys between buildings to deter against potential snipers from taking pot-shots.

We could not see any uniformed personnel in the neighbourhood as most checkpoints were being manned by civilian militias with AKs. They were often middle-aged men dressed in soviet era leather jackets standing at traffic junctions in makeshift checkpoints created by parking several cars perpendicularly across the road.

We still waited for the traffic lights before crossing the road though, and really appreciated the warm sunlight and safety in numbers. Until I realised that I was the only person wearing a white jacket among a group of darkly dressed shoppers.

There was already a sizeable queue outside the supermarket as it was going to open in a few minutes. Luckily, the queue started to move as soon as we joined it. I scanned the loading bay in the carpark for signs of supply trucks but couldn't see any. I assumed that some of the more courageous drivers would have taken up arms and gone to join the fight, so we were likely buying whatever was in storage.

The automatic doors were no longer sliding as everyone entered through the swing-out side door for crowd control. On the door hung a notice with the shortened operating hours until 3pm as the next curfew would start at 5pm. I was confident about our food supplies at home, so I just grabbed a shopping basket and headed straight for some fresh produce. The sight of fruits and vegetables on display was rather reassuring considering the situation. People were quickly trying to buy the things they needed, so they remained orderly and there wasn't any elbow fighting.

While I was waiting in line for the self-service weighing machine, three Ukrainian reservist soldiers with weapons slung over the shoulders were pushing a trolley full of groceries to the front of the queue. They politely asked if they could bypass the queue as they needed to return to their stations as soon as possible.

The lady who was about to weigh her cabbage placed it back into her shopping trolley and took the bag of oranges from the soldiers' trolley. "Certainly," she replied and weighed the fruits for the soldier. "*Slava Ukraïni!* Glory to Ukraine!" Others in the queue were shouting as they looked on. Every shopper in the fresh produce section echoed loudly, "*Heroyam Slava!* Glory to the heroes!"

Looking at the contents inside the soldiers' trolley – mostly snacks like cookies, bread, drinks and fruits – I assumed they were still well stocked with army rations. I am a firm believer of how little pick-me-ups like these can sustain people during dreadful durations.

Unlike movie scenarios designed to instil panic by dramatising shoppers fighting one another, what I experienced was very much the opposite. In fact, people were now kinder towards each other compared to during times of peace. One shopper had offered to help me select the correct vegetable itemisation for my red chilli at the weighing machine because I appeared to be struggling as I scrolled

Truly grateful to the dedicated delivery drivers who braved Russian attacks just to deliver fresh produce

through the long weighing list. It was already tricky when an item's description was handwritten in cursive Cyrillic, but the weighing machine monitor displayed a digital version. Somewhere along the digitisation of Cyrillic alphabets, there was a leap of understanding that everyone practiced Cyrillic penmanship.

Even the counter promoters were eager to push their discounted items, explaining that in their decade-long careers, they had never seen such a slashing of prices. President Zelensky made it a punishable offence for anyone caught profiteering by unlawful price-jacking during the invasion. So from what I was witnessing, it seemed like local producers were trying to out-discount their competitors in a show of corporate patriotism.

The smell of freshly baked bread wafted over from the delicatessen section. The whiff of Maillard reactions with sugar caramelisation concocted a flashback similar to that in the animation film *Ratatouille*. I was suddenly transported back to my childhood, standing on the uneven, uprooted dark red tiles of my neighbourhood, hiding from the hot afternoon sun under a large tree waiting for the freshly baked pointy baguette loaves. By the next blink, I was back in the supermarket wishing for a jar of *kaya*, or coconut jam, to fall from the sky while waiting in line for the bread.

The bakers were in overdrive as they fired all the ovens, modern electrical ones and the traditional torne, or tandoor. They were too busy to wipe the sweat from their foreheads, engrossed in making bread for the people in their winter jackets standing at the counter.

By the time I picked up a fresh loaf, the queue from the cashier had already stretched beyond the bakery at the opposite end of the supermarket. Not wanting to buy beyond the storage capacity of my refrigerator, I decided to join the cashier's queue intersecting with the bread queue. After over one and a half hours of standing in line, I was finally near the cashier. I realised it was also time for me to take my attention away from my phone.

As I looked around, I spotted rows and rows of empty shelves at the liquor section. Elsewhere in the supermarket, there were various degree of product shortages. Bread flour had not been restocked, canned vegetables were left with only one selection of beans. But they were usually replenished by a single brand or an encroachment of products from another section, so no shelf was left empty.

However, in the liquor section, empty shelves were laid bare. My first thought was that most of those liquors were not flammable enough to be used for Molotov cocktails. The situation also did not feel desperate enough to pour away good wine just to use the bottles.

I only found out the reason for that after joining my group of waiting neighbours warming themselves in the sun outside the supermarket. The sale of alcohol was banned during martial law because the policing of alcohol misdemeanors would be an unnecessary use of public security manpower.

I remember during my first snowboarding trip to the Carpathians mountains, two gentlemen from the table next to mine were offering me vodka before I could even tuck into my breakfast. Even Natalia's grandmother is known for her potent homemade moonshine, самогон. Tasty food and alcohol are very much a part of Ukrainian life. But for the moment, it was better for everyone to be sober than sad.

I crashed straight onto the yoga mat after returning from the shopping trip. We woke up slightly after noon to organise our refrigerator. We had maxed out all available space and still had some fresh supplies left out in the open.

Fortunately, the balcony was still usable as the temperature was still cold, but we may unknowingly be creating a buffet for the crows. The wisdom of practices passed down from Natalia grandfather helped to point us in the right direction again. He was a former activist who had survived the Siberian Gulag during the Soviet era. They were the first generation of Ukrainians that explored the concept of a national identity which did not sit well with the Soviet government when Stalin was in charge.

Natalia explained that the most effective way of storing our fresh supplies would be to boil them before cutting it into small pieces, and then stored into zip lock bags that can be stuffed into the crevices in-between other frozen stuff. It was a wonderful problem-solving solution as long as we had electricity. Because we did not prepare any canning jars and caps to can our own food.

Off the grid survival techniques may look exotic in those online videos but with no means of food production while living within a power grid, we will be like trapped animals in an abandoned zoo.

Losing electricity meant that all communication would be lost. I noticed the unstable service of our wifi as reports of server attacks and reboots have been ongoing from before the invasion. I had already written down on paper the important contact numbers and emails, but decided to install a low bandwidth chat app recommended by Ukrainian hackers on my spare phone as a form of back-up. We heard of people losing cellular data networks in Russian-occupied areas. Since I was not involved in maritime, I didn't have a satellite phone around either.

From the beginning of the invasion, we had seen plenty of online footage of the carnage and destruction by countless uploaders. But when a friend sent a selfie taken in front of an unexploded missile, the proximity of the ruin made the hair on the back of my neck stand. Our friend Misha was showing us the spot where a failed missile had landed. What was shocking to us was that the signpost which the missile had impacted was on the sidewalk we strolled with Misha just a week ago.

A week ago, we were just discussing staying or leaving with Misha at a Chinese hot pot restaurant that was within walking distance from his home. Now he was ready to take his family to the rural areas south of the city. He did not have a weekend cottage in the outskirts and was just going to cramp his wife, child and pets into someone else's compound, and live communally with other families that had taken refuge there. I suppose that it was too unnerving to live within 10 kilometres of an airport.

We wished him Godspeed as everyone understood that the Russians were trying to encircle Kyiv. While the survivors

IX SHEN

Seasons changes and mood swings – snowfall, sunshine and freezing temperatures in a day.

inside the city were trying to cope with the challenges of trying to stay alive without losing sanity, the media were constantly posting footage of the long Russian convoy approaching Kyiv which had grown to 60 kilometres in length by then. Staying put in Kyiv during those moments was like being in being in a lunette where the rails of the guillotine were made by under-qualified carpenters as the blade was constantly falling and stopping intermittently. The ever present, but awkwardly mentioned, Russian nuclear arsenal was just fanning the fire of the pressure cooker housing everything.

If anyone asks what the logic to all these was, my conclusion would be that our sense of logic had become a weakness for the demented to exploit.

Remaining sane during insane times is challenging as we had to constantly remind ourselves that whatever we had assumed to be the norm during peaceful times, could be weaponised and used against us. For with the sanity of a moral high ground, we should not be capable of reliving those barbaric dark ages again.

Having absorbed my fill of negative news, I decided to get some fresh air from the stairway after dinner. Against the background of the blackout city, I could see specks of white snow drifting down from the overcast sky. I have seen snow covering the landscape of the countryside when it snowed for hours. Even with heated windshield wipers and deicing fluid, it would be difficult to see the sides of the road as a vehicle moves forward against the horizontal flying snowflakes.

I could not imagine how a tank driver would be able to navigate through the periscope or what a frostbitten tank commander might be able to see through his goggles. The last time I snowboarded in a blizzard, I fell into a ravine. Somehow it felt like even nature has chosen its side on this conflict. Sensing that it would be a rather quiet night, we took the risk of spending the night in our wardrobe instead of the basement carpark.

Instinct vs Rationality

WAKING UP ON a March morning to a snow-covered city was a bittersweet delight. It was not uncommon to encounter heavy snowfall in March. In fact, I knew of a spot in the Carpathians mountains where the melted snow would form a small lake which you can slide from snow to water in a single descend.

The latest update we had regarding the Russian encirclement of Kyiv was that they were somewhere between crawling from a freeze and grinding to a halt. Under the current weather conditions, for any large convoy to maintain progress, the logistical operations had become deadly important. We could only console ourselves with internet fables of Ukrainian thieves who stole a "Z" marked fuel truck from the convoy only to discover that it was empty.

Apparently, corruption was so rampant that the fuel which was destined for the front line had already been siphoned off into the black market. That made another video about expired seven-year-old military rations look minuscule in the scale of corporate corruption. We understood that incidents like these were not going to stop the Russian war machine, but it perked us up and helped us to deal with our upturned lives. Resilience is so dependent on mental strength.

For breakfast, we could just pour cold milk over granola or put in extra effort to accomplish an eggs benedict without the English muffins. That re-channelling of focus seems absurd, but it became highly fulfilling to complete the entire process. Perhaps the risk of an air raid interruption made it even more enticing to be able to serve up a decent breakfast.

It was therapeutic to perform simplistic daily rituals to help ease our minds from the onslaught of negative information. Natalia busied herself with the cleaning chores, especially with to our cats' addiction to catnip. I suspected Natalia unconsciously enjoyed the drama of nagging and cleaning up their vomit. There had to be something mystical to why movies portray Asian monks in a mystical, Zen-like state when they are sweeping the temple grounds, but I have seen them busy checking their phones beneath those robes as well.

There was a sudden buzz of messages in our apartment's chatgroup – one neighbour reported seeing a man jump onto a balcony to one of the units. We checked that all our windows were bolted and went down to the security office to better understand the situation. A small group had already gathered by the time we arrived, we understood that from the security footage, no one was seen approaching or leaving our building that morning. But all the security cameras were covering the perimeter of the building on the street level. No one would be pointing a security camera towards the sky to monitor the vertical sides of the building.

The suspicious person was seen jumping onto one of the balconies in the middle floors from the rooftop of the abandoned building next to ours. We knew that more than half the units were empty as their occupiers had already fled Kyiv. The security guard's protocol was to physically inspect the premises for signs of suspicious activities before notifying the already stretched police force.

One security guard needed to monitor the screens to see if the person is spotted on camera again, which meant that we had to form a neighbourhood watch together with our remaining security guard to check on the empty units. In the gathering of mostly ladies with children, I was the only man available. So Natalia and I volunteered to tag along with our unarmed security guard to patrol our building.

After knocking on the doors of our neighbours to check that no one was speaking under duress, we approached the level where the suspicious person had reportedly been seen. It was a vacant corner unit with a balcony within jumping distance to the roof of the next building for a bold person. The other two families living on the same level did not see or hear anything suspicious.

The trio of us stood outside the apartment's door at a loss for the next course of action. The security guard did not have the key to open the door and it would not make sense for us to knock. Natalia opened the window in the common corridor and attempted to look into the vacant unit. Without informing us, she slipped through the window and lunged for the apartment's balcony.

Our shocked security guard stared at me in disbelief while I shrugged my shoulders. I had to explain that Natalia was a former member of Odesa city's speed climbing team. Judging from his age and the size of belly, I didn't think he would be following after us as I went after Natalia through the open window.

Stepping across from the window onto the ledge of the balcony was a relatively easy stride for the length of my legs. I just had to remind myself of the three-point contact rule when free climbing. Natalia had already scaled onto another balcony by the time I caught sight of her.

I couldn't shout for her to stop. Not because of the danger of scaling from balcony to balcony, but from the danger in the way she was checking the windows. She was presenting herself as an easy target for anyone looking outwards.

I had to grab her by the arm to get her attention and it probably dawned upon her by the time I pulled her down to hide behind the low wall beneath the window to whisper how risky her actions had been.

Trying to confront an intruder unarmed was purely instinctive behaviour, while I understood Natalia confrontational motive when someone intrudes on our turf. I was also aware that there wasn't much we could do except to surprise the intruder. I demonstrated how to peep tactically and move from cover to cover while we checked for signs of forced entries. But there was only so much we could do with unaided eyes and ears.

Satisfied that everything appeared to be normal, we climbed our way back towards the common corridor. As we discussed the situation with our security guard, we understood that there had been reports of saboteurs spray painting or marking buildings as potential aerial targets. We decided that the best way to be sure was to check our rooftop.

We knew the top floor neighbours had fled, leaving the entire level empty and a few vacant units with unfinished renovations. If the intruder was as professional as we had imagined, then an empty unit with uncompleted renovations would be ideal to hide as there wouldn't be any risk of home security cameras.

There were dusty footprints leading in and out from one of the vacant unit's door.

But they were most likely from the renovation workers as our cleaning services had stopped working since the invasion begun. The lift chimed suddenly to announce the arrival of our very own neighbourhood militia. He was staying on another level and had been performing roadblock duties elsewhere when he saw our chatgroup and rushed back to our apartment to help.

The presence of a loaded weapon helped to ease my mind a little. He tried to open the door, but it was locked, so he banged on the door of the empty unit and shouted his authority under martial law. Everyone waited tensely in silence.

After banging several times without any replies, we were left scratching our heads again. We were desperately trying to reach the owner of the unit who was somewhere at the border with Poland and phone signals were intermittent. While they were trying to discuss the pros and cons of breaking down the door, I noticed dusty handprints on the door handle of unit next door. I highlighted it to Natalia and she studied them for a while before reaching for the handle and opening the door.

The militia guy went in with his weapon drawn and told me to back him up. Puzzled, I showed Natalia my bare palms and followed him into the unit, squatting behind the nearest pillar from the door to scan the surroundings.

The owner had actually bought both units and were renovating them into one. Without any curtains, the sunlight from the windows lit the whole place. There were piles of renovation materials all over the unit. The stacks of cement were closest to me while another pile of ceramic tiles leaned against one wall. Huge spools of insulating foam were standing in another corner.

I was wondering how we were going to clear the place when the militia guy shouted his presence and authority while walking towards the windows. He turned around and saw me squatting behind the pillar and waved for me to get closer.

Instinctively, I found myself unable to straighten up to walk but crouched from my pillar towards a pile of construction wood. Unfortunately for me, those were just huge rectangular plywood boards with nothing I could grab single-handedly.

Anyone who has experienced close-quarters battle with either paintballs or virtual gaming should know that every corner and blind spot will just send your adrenaline pumping to the maximum limitations of your capillaries. This was one of those moments I wished I had registered for a firearms license when there was the opportunity to do so.

Being unarmed, the only thing I could do was to cover my point man's blind spot by being as close as possible to his blind spot – while hoping that any weapon that presents itself would be aiming at my point man. Hopefully.

We might have seen the fancy moves of a hero disarming an assailant in the movies, and I have even mucked around on sets with weapons instructors trying to snatch someone's weapon. But I suspect that anyone who has been trained in scaling tall buildings to perform sabotage for coordinated aerial attacks would not be holding the weapon that would be vulnerable to a snatch. All I had were handfuls of renovation dust and a deep breath.

We had almost cleared all the rooms in the units when Natalia came in for a look around. I didn't even know how to begin explaining the risks of her action before she noticed a makeshift wooden construction ladder which was leading up to the rooftop terrace and wandered towards it. She asked why the window was ajar.

We gathered at the foot of the ladder and stared up the unclosed window silently as our imagination wandered. Our militia guy was younger than our security guard but of a similar physique, so everyone eyed the flimsy nailed-up ladder solemnly. As before, Natalia went up the ladder as point person, opened the window and jumped out of view.

I supposed it would not be proper for me to ask for his weapon, so I went after Natalia before the ladder had finished wobbling from her ascend. It was a small drop from the window down to the rooftop, but it was good to be breathing fresh air after wandering around a unit undergoing renovation.

I stopped Natalia from scaling onto another terrace not because she would be needing to climb onto the outer ledge of the roof, but I explained the risks of performing such actions unarmed. She was squatting on roof ledge contemplating when we heard our militia guy dropping onto the terrace.

Stepping in Snow to Find a Plum Blossom

WE WERE STUDYING the layout of the rooftop terraces to devise a feasible search plan when I highlighted that we were likely the only people to have come up because all the footprints in the snow were made by us. It had been snowing since last night and the report of the intruder only came that morning. So all we had to do was to walk along the perimeter of the outer ledge to search for footprints.

So we climbed onto the outer ledge and went searching from one terrace to another. Since the entire floor was vacant, we took the opportunity to check out the various decoration concepts of our neighbours as well. We went three-quarters around the building without spotting anything suspicious until the outer ledge ran into a high wall.

I could see some water tank structures behind that high wall so I assumed that it must lead to the utilities segment of our building. The wall was more than twice a man's height and I couldn't find any footprints of attempted scaling. Unless our intruder brought a pole for vaulting over the high wall, we could conclude that we had cleared all the terraces along the roof.

Feeling relieved and rather silly to have allowed our imagination to run free, we joked about our neighbour's décor as we retraced our steps back towards the window which we had leapt from. As we gathered near the window discussing whose shoulder we should be stepping on to climb back to the window, I decided to try looking around for outdoor furniture that we might borrow from any of our unsuspecting neighbours.

I spotted a wooden crate at the far end of the rooftop and walked towards it. It was where the outer ledge merged with the opposite end of the high wall. But unlike the other end, at this end I could peek around the side of the high wall, so I leaned outwards to take a look.

I could feel the hair on the back of my neck standing up when I looked into the utilities section. In the pristine white snow were darkish footprints of a single person, the direction of travel was from a door towards another area of the utilities section which I could not see around the high wall. I turned around and placed my index finger to my lips while waving for Natalia and militia man to join me.

No explanation was required when they saw the footprints. Since there was a service door to access the rooftop utilities, we decided to take photos of the area to verify with the security guard would it have been possible for service personnel to perform routine work on our roof during the military invasion.

Our security guard was waiting for us at the entrance of the empty unit when we showed him the picture with the footprints in the snow. We were actually disappointed when he told us that all cleaning and maintenance services had been halted since the beginning of the invasion. Only the security service was still in operation. In fact, our security team had not had the opportunity to return home since the start of the invasion.

With that new information, we knew that we had to inspect those footprints on the utilities segment of our roof and asked our security guard for directions to that service door. The service door had to be accessed through another fire escape stairway which was only accessible through the lower floors. Because all access on the top floor which we were currently at had been sealed.

Everyone had to descend a level and walk across the common corridor to another fire escape in order to reach the service door to the roof. I took the opportunity of our detour to sprint down to our apartment to grab my selfie stick. I did not have high hopes for the structural strength of the selfie stick to be used as a weapon, but I had other plans for it with my 360-degree camera.

We stepped back onto the roof of our building after the security guard unlocked the service door with a key. We could see the set of footprints of a person wandering about on the roof because the snow had not begun to melt at the area directly in front of the door. However, the snow had already melted in the other sections of the rooftop service area, so we couldn't tell where the person might have wandered.

I told Natalia and our elderly security guard to stay by the door as I followed the militia man to clear the service area. There were not that many blind spots or corners among the service area as there was just a few maintenance switch boxes

Undeniable signs of a trespasser

Seeking out hiding spots along the rooftop

installed at different walls of the area. We cleared the area rather quickly since there were no signs of forced entry. But if our intruder could pick the lock of the service door, I doubt we would be able to find any signs of forced entry as well.

The only places we had not checked were the top of the water tanks and lift motors rooms. There was a steel ladder bolted against the wall running parallel with the lighting conductor. I explained to the militia man that I will have to take point since I would be able to peer over the top ledge with my 360 camera on the selfie stick and he would be better off providing cover from below the ladder.

I climbed to the top of the ladder as noiselessly as I could and swung outwards to plaster myself against the wall. I extended my selfie stick with the 360-degree camera as far away from the ladder as possible while looking at the wireless live feed on my phone at the same time.

The rooftop was empty. I swung back onto the ladder and climbed over the ledge to step onto the small rooftop. I signalled that there was nothing suspicious to the others below. Only then did I notice the panoramic view from our rooftop.

We were not the tallest building in the vicinity, as there were clearly higher rooftops around me. Neither could I see anything strategic from our vantage point except for the bridge which had experienced a brief fire fight.

It was not logical to attack the bridge if the Russians were planning to use it for rolling their tanks into the capital and even less logical to operate a laser marker from our roof as the saboteur would be exposing himself to any Ukrainian anti-snipers on the other higher rooftops around us.

The illogical logic of this invasion can be quite mind-boggling at times.

In the end we concluded that either our roof had a phantom dodging our dramatic opera, or some homeless person was taking shelter during the night and left in the morning after it had stopped snowing.

Because we would have been described as the Tang dynasty poet who braved heavy snow in hopes of chancing upon a plum blossom to inspire the poetry composition 踏雪寻梅 – for without a bloom, it was much ado about nothing.

Surviving Sanity

THE AIR STRIKES during the early hours of the morning were one of the more intensive ones we experienced. I suppose the Russians were trying to provide as much air cover as possible while their troops were attempting to encircle the city in the snow, or they were stuck in the snow while attempting to encircle the city.

Whenever the intensity picks up in a fight, we can never tell if it was driven by strategy or desperation, as those constantly interchange.

But when we saw the reports of the Russians attacking the largest nuclear power plant of Europe near Zaporizhzhia, I was beginning to suspect that desperation was the strategy. The Chernobyl incident may have already been dramatised into a television series, but I could still remember vividly the low-resolution news footage I saw back in 1986. And Zaporizhzhia is nearly twice as powerful.

It was challenging to wrap my head around the sanity of the military action unless all nuclear plants were meant to be strikable targets as long as it served the overall strategy. So leaving sanity aside temporarily, unless the overall strategy was to reduce Ukraine into a nuclear waste land, it was quite incomprehensible to understand the attack on a nuclear power plant.

If I were to indulge that imaginative insanity, then Kremlin was planning to shoo away the people who disagreed with them by bulldozing into Ukraine while kicking up as much dust as they could. Followed by the installation of a puppet president to do their bidding.

It was a page out from the Mongolian playbook when they conquered the land of Rus and installed Ivan I of Muscovy to collect taxes on behalf of the Golden Horde back in 13th century. The only differences being that during this age of information, they will probably be checking social media posts instead of measuring the captive's height against a cartwheel.

Having outlived the Soviet Union, the Ukrainians passionately cherish the freedom of their future generations. They know that the only way for the invaders to succeed was over their dead bodies, literally. What the rest of the world had to ponder over was – do we still want to trade with the horde?

As the media all over the world were being flooded by countless uploads of the Ukrainian development in almost real time. I noticed an undeniable rift between the reports from different regions of the world. Almost everyone was regurgitating from the same sources on the ground – most likely to be Ukrainian – since there were only a handful of foreign correspondents near the frontline.

It was a dumbfounding experience to witness the disparity of people's reactions to the same situation, that would range from utter astonishment to cynical rejoicing of the Ukrainians plight. Some people wanted the truth while others rejected it blatantly. But what was really bone-chilling was that many preferred not to know. I think ignorance can be only blissful when have you have it, not when you choose it.

With so many peaceful lives upturned, forgiving and forgetting had become overbearing burdens on everyone's faith.

Despite church bells being drowned out by air raid sirens, the Ukrainians were still preparing pancakes for the Maslynstna Pancake Festival traditionally celebrated before Lent.

The dishevelment of our own emotions as we tried to cope with everything while attempting to survive with sanity, was like being encapsulated inside a lump of flour floating on the pancake batter, trying frantically to swirl away from those high speed mixers.

We were grateful for the internet to be operating so we could seek refuge by watching online videos of fireplaces whist listening to wooden logs crackling. But I have to admit that the Youtube series of Hitler's rants were good for releasing tension, as it felt like I was looking at myself through a twisted periscope with multiple prisms, reflective and fuzzy, real but also unreal.

Our isolation bubble was pricked when we heard a polite knocking on our door. The neighbourhood volunteers made up of 2014 Euromaidan veterans were going round the area to see if everyone was alright while collecting empty bottles.

They were organising a Molotov cocktail making party.

The most traumatised pancakes I had ever made

Taking Out the Trash

I NOTICED THAT there hadn't been any fresh supplies in the supermarkets in the last grocery run after the curfew was lifted. The supermarket had been emptying their storage to fill up the shelves with an ever-decreasing variety of choices.

With the status of the Russian encirclement, I doubt fresh grocery supplies would be able to make its way into the capital. We were still decently stocked up in terms of supplies, but when the fresh produces stopped appearing, we knew we had entered into another stage of the battle.

We were prepared to stay put under the theory that any military operation would be coming to a swift conclusion, it was the duration which we had to endure. But when our friend from Irpin reported that the departed Russian tanks had reappeared in their neighbourhood, the concept of duration was getting more difficult to grasp.

Several towns outside of Kyiv have been occupied by the invaders. With internet and electricity getting cut off, residents were resorting to chopping wood to stay warm and prepare meals. I remembered feeling the volley of artillery shells being fired on my way back from the supermarket. I could not tell which side the shelling were coming from, but I could feel the force from the energy that were passing through the air and ground with every explosion.

Psychologically, fears are classified as innate or acquired. What I was feeling was definitely innate even though I was kilometres away. I could not imagine the shell shock for the people on the receiving end if they were lucky enough to have a hole to dive into.

By the time I got back to the apartment, our cats had voluntarily climbed into their carriers for a sense of security. Natalia was very nervous about the current situation as well.

Even though there was no warning of an air raid, we decided to head down to the bunker just in case. That was one of those moments that calming music would not be able to drown out the explosions. While we were resting underground, we tried to gather as much information about the encirclement as possible.

Collectively among the neighbours, we understood the closest reported sightings of the invaders from Kyiv had been around 30 kilometres away. Taking cover from intermittent air strikes was already unpleasant enough. But if the artillery could get to be within range of the city, the psychological trauma of bracing barrage after barrage could be unnecessarily damaging.

We understood the Ukrainian defenders were using land as a means of defence by thinning out the invaders for counter attacks. But to be waiting stationary as they spread around the city while attacking at the same time was mentally taxing.

We were grateful that our community had never lost faith that the invaders would never be victorious. Everyone had become extra caring and helpful to keep the *kampong* spirit alive.

I remember seeing two Ukrainian army trucks speeding across a bridge on a bright clear day. With the intense fighting spreading from Hostomel to Moschun, I was surprised that they did not choose to drive at night, unless the urgency of the situation warranted the risk of Russian aerial attacks on their supply trucks.

But what made those truck memorable was that the driver of the front truck had missed the exit while the driver of the second truck had braked in the middle of the bridge. He was blowing his horn urgently to call out to the truck in front. The second driver swung right to exit from the bridge and sped away. What happened later was that a few passengers from a civilian car that had stopped behind the trucks got out from their car and spread across the bridge.

The passengers stopped any oncoming traffic from their position while one passenger was waving for the first truck to reverse back towards them. I saw the front truck reverse back into view and stopped beside the coordinating passenger. The driver was asking for directions and the passengers were helping to orient him to the city. I could see the driver looked clearly like a reservist soldier with undersized uniform and balding hair. He was likely not from Kyiv as he was rather unfamiliar with the network of the city roadways. He got a general direction from the passengers and sped off in pursuit of the other truck.

Strays accomodating eateries in Ukraine are a common sight, although bullets are not welcome.

    I knew the direction of that road led towards the Irpin bridge which had been demolished earlier during the invasion. From the truck size and drivers' urgency, my guess would be that they were most likely to be on an ammo run. It takes courage for a civilian reservist driver to undertake the task of frontline ammunitions delivery under broad daylight because they become the easiest target if spotted from the air and all those passing passengers who had helped to redirect the truck on that bridge were placing themselves at risk as well.

That was '*kampong* spirit' at its finest.

That was how I view the underlying drive behind the phenomenal strength of the Ukrainians fighting off this invasion. No one was in denial about the military numbers of the invaders, but everyone was willing to stand up to them.

From the gallant soldiers fighting on the frontline to the selfless disregard for personal safety of utilities repairmen, to thrill seeking amateur drone operators performing reconnaissance missions and volunteer housewives cooking for members of the militia – there was even the legend of an old Ukrainian lady who eliminated an entire squad of Russian soldiers by offering them meat pies laced with rat poison.

By then, I had already began reporting the situation in Kyiv for the Singapore news on a nightly basis. At the same time, I was getting a lot of requests for interviews by different media organisations as well. I remember that was a request for an interview which I suggested be scheduled in the afternoon Ukraine time. But the media was hoping to conduct the interview in the morning due to the different time zones.

It was a necessary knock to my head, as only then did I realise how most people outside of Ukraine would not be able to relate to the state we were in.

News about the Ukraine situation had become the most watched reality show. It was mostly images of destruction and suffering, which was simple to understand and could transcend across screens. But the strength everyone was mustering to maintain that dignified sanity, while contributing to the fight without being killed or injured, was something which had to be experienced and not watched.

IX SHEN

I had to explain to the person who requested for the interview that the mornings hours of Kyiv were best spent sleeping as those precious hours after air raids were usually most uneventful. Meaning that we would be able to catch a few hours of rest without much fear of any sudden disruptions of running into the underground shelter. It was not reasonable for us to expect people outside of Ukraine to be able to understand our situation.

For us, the process from contemplation to determination, and then to action, had been turbulent and blunt. Countless stories of humankind's ability to adapt and survive have been told throughout our collective history. But for the people who are not involved, the stages of shock, denial, anger, depression, acceptance and integration have been skipped, and presumptions are made based on whatever information is presented. I had a new-found admiration for scientists who could compound their field of studies into bite sides intrigues for the common audience because reality is multi-faceted.

With the imminent threat of attack on Kyiv closing around the city, everyone was worried about when the Russian tanks will start rolling into the neighbourhood.

That night, I heard some heavy vehicle driving up next to our building. The rumbling of its engine was especially loud as the streets have been silent since curfew. Because our windows had been barricaded by then, the only way to check on the vehicle was to peep from the fire escape stairway.

I felt my way in the dark because I did not want to turn on my headlamp and highlight my presence. I crouched towards the edge of the stairway and tried to listen to any sound coming from below. I heard wheels clattering over tiled pavement as something heavy was being pushed. I stood up slowly to risk a glance down. Working with just the brake lights of their vehicles, the waste collectors were clearing out the dumpsters of our building.

The Ukrainians were still taking out the trash.

Gasping in a Vacuum

WHEN THE RUSSIAN army previously crossed the border into the eastern region of Ukraine, everyone accepted the escalation of the intensity for the fighting in the Donbas region without much hype. It had been going on for eight years. But when the invaders crossed into Ukraine from the Belarus border, the world was shocked to see that the Kyiv had become the target.

Those who were staying in the city understood that it meant that the Kremlin wanted to decapitate the Ukrainian government to achieve their goals. But it was obvious that the Ukrainian defenders had no intention of letting that happen. Recalling how the Russian army used artillery to pound Chechen's capital city of Grozny into submission, we had to ask ourselves if we were truly ready for that.

It would mean hiding in our underground shelter for extensive periods of time or even moving to the deeper metro stations if our building suffers damages. But the most worrisome of all was that we did not have any access to double-chambered bunkers with filtration system to take cover from thermobaric or chemical bombs.

Top: Descending more than 300 feet underground for safety or to catch a train

Left: Strength in geometry – arcs, arcs and more arcs

Brutal destruction of a residential building

We only had a few more days before those artillery would be creeping within firing range. Despite the sense of relief we felt every time there was a report of Russian equipment being destroyed, we understood that the Ukrainians were heavily reliant on US-supplied Javelins to counter the Russian advance.

Our plight was dependent on whichever side could resupply faster. We decided that we not only had to be on standby 24/7 to run down into our underground shelter, but we also had to be on standby for any evacuation opportunity to escape from the Kyiv encirclement as well.

One of the sources of information which I had been using to monitor the situation was the official Wechat account of the Chinese embassy in Ukraine. Unlike embassies of many countries that had closed after releasing evacuation notices telling their own citizens leave the country. The Chinese embassy was just reminding their citizens to remain in safe shelters and abide by the local emergency laws.

I believed that due to the close bilateral relationship between China and Russia, they would be communicating closely to prevent another incident like Belgrade 1999 from happening. So when I saw the Wechat posting from the Chinese embassy about instructions on how to meet for their scheduled evacuation, I guessed the Chinese diplomats might have received information regarding the indiscriminate shelling to come.

With reports of the invaders firing onto the humanitarian corridors after ceasefire had been negotiated, it would be suicidal for us to evacuate without a sustainable ceasefire. We had friends hiding out in the rural areas about 30 kilometres south of the city. They believed the southern regions would be safe and pleaded for us to get as far away from Kyiv as possible. They were a family of three squeezing into a single room of a large farmhouse with 12 different families living under one roof. Everyone had to compromise and live together with relative harmony, except when fights broke out between unfamiliar pets encroaching over each other's territory.

There have been reports of civilian cars being shot at by the invaders while the residents were trying to escape from the fighting. Some have been accidental but many were because the invaders wanted to rob the refugees of their imported cars.

The railway tracks had also been struck by Russian rockets, but the Ukrainian railway workers have been constantly repairing the damages with a lot of courage under fire. To leave Kyiv, there were so many options from every direction. Too many, in fact. Information from those who had already left or were planning to leave were also contradictory at times.

We had seen reports of sixteen passengers stuffed into a train wagon meant to sleep four, with their luggage abandoned on station platforms as they could only carry whatever that could place on their laps for twenty hours. Aisle seats meant seating onto the aisle. The train schedules had became unpredictably erratic.

So we concluded that if we were to make a run for it, it should be towards the western part of Ukraine with a minimum distance of 500 kilometres away, where we would not be under any immediate threat of attack from Russian ground troops. Anywhere nearer and we may end up in a worse situation if the battlefield was to shift abruptly.

The supplies we had stocked inside our apartment would be enough to last us for months, including our cats. If we were to evacuate, our food security on the run will be a big unknown because we would only be able to buy whatever might still be left in the stores along our evacuation route. So we narrowed down a list of potential cities and started searching for local contacts with the most current information.

We did not choose Poland at that moment because we did not want to be faced with the choice of abandoning our cats at border. Poland had already waived negative COVID tests and quarantines requirements for anyone seeking entry from Ukraine since the second day of the invasion. But the European Union had very stringent regulations for bringing in pets and we didn't have any confirmation as to whether those regulations had been waived for pets as well.

Our cats were scheduled to go for their annual vaccinations due to expire early March. We had made appointments for them for 28th February but the invasion on the 24th had made all the veterinary clinics ceased their operations. We had seen social media posts of pets being abandoned inside their carriers out in the snow while their owners crossed into Poland on foot. The volunteers helping on the Ukrainian side of the border were pleading for people to take in abandoned pets. So if we were to keep the option of going into Poland open, our cats will need to get access to an internationally recognised veterinary clinic that could administer those vaccinations.

Packing for our underground shelter had already become a daily routine. I just assumed that to pack for an evacuation would be just like an expanded version of what we had been packing daily. But when I factored in the components that we would need to give up – the kitchen, fridge, washing machine, cat toilets and running water – I was suddenly at a loss about what not to pack.

Hiding, living, eating and sleeping in our walk-in wardrobe

THE THIRD WEEK

Journeying into the unknown

Starting Blocks

AFTER DAYS WITHOUT fresh grocery supplies, I was elated to see fresh green apples in the fruit section. But those under ripe green apples were the only fresh produce to make it past the encirclement, most of the other shelves had not been restocked.

The COVID lockdowns may have placed restrictions on personal movements, but the variety and amount of food were never in jeopardy. We could only worship the committed transportation drivers who were delivering apples in the midst of combat, knowing that there won't be any insurance under writing for them. But we could not presume that they would continue these deliveries throughout the invasion. Preparing for our food and water supplies to be cut off was one thing, witnessing the cutting off was another.

I shared the good news of fresh apples with Natalia, but when she saw how under ripe they were, she understood it was a forced harvest due to the current circumstances. City

Green with envy

folk like me are envious of people who spent their childhood growing up with vegetable gardens and fruit trees. They can deduce so much information from any fruit or vegetable.

Natalia had received information from a friend in Lviv about a flat for rental, he would try reserving it for us if we could get ourselves to Lviv. We agreed that Lviv would be a safe choice as we would be out of the encirclement, and could make further plans after getting there.

But without any sustainable ceasefire in place, any refugee on the run would be prone to attack. It did not matter which side was shooting at you. It only mattered which side came into proximity with you.

To plan for evacuation during an invasion, one needed to understand the philosophy of the 1981 arcade game Frogger. The situation is fluid and constantly moving in a variety of directions. One can make all the risk assessments to reach the desired destination, but after leaping or landing on any of those moving parts, it might still boil down to fate in the end.

The trains to Lviv were still running – a 12-hour journey which should be quite manageable even for our cats. We checked online for the earliest available ticket to purchase but all seats were sold out for the whole week.

We were naïve to think that we could buy a whole coupé for our cats and ourselves. We later found out from another friend who took a nearly 40-hour train ride to Romania with her grandmother that they were part of a group of twelve adults with eight children inside one sleeper wagon meant for four. Everyone was stepping over each other, and with the nonstop wailing of the young children, it was an experience to be avoided, if possible. One station was even struck by rockets after their departure.

I was beginning to give up on the train option when Natalia said she will call her mother for help. Her mother has a close personal friend working in the Ukrainian railway. I was hesitant but continued to pack for our train journey while we waited to hear from her mother.

We had travelled on Ukrainian trains before There were plenty of stairs to climb within the Kyiv station and the entrance into the train was rather narrow with a large height difference from the platform. Some smaller stations had platforms shorter than the length of the train, forcing passengers to jump onto the tracks on arrival. With our hands full carrying the pet carriers, backpacks were the default choice for lugging all our belongings.

We had been told that the supermarkets in Lviv were still well stocked, so we should be able to replenish most of our necessities if we could just get into the city.

I had almost finished packing our backpacks when Natalia's mother called. She told us that there was an unscheduled train being organised that very night – an emergency evacuation freight arranged for the people fleeing Kyiv. Due to the risk of rocket attacks, unlike most trains departing from the central station, this train had to be boarded from a maintenance station in another part of the city. But the only passengers allowed on the train were women and children only. We did not want to discuss the option of us travelling separately, as neither of us were keen to voyage into the unknown with the extra burden of worrying about each other.

We has watched videos of male foreign students being denied entry into trains as there were just too many women and children trying to leave. Even single fathers had to entrust their children to other female passengers to get their children out of the city. During a mass exodus of women and children, the priorities of men and pets were just not as high, and I had no intention of finding out who was the lower of the two.

Personally, I would rather avoid the train if we could. I had been caught in oxygen depriving passenger jams during peak travel season in China before, spending hours zig-zagging a few hundred metres inside confined spaces. I could only imagine the potential of a stampede if an explosion were to go off near the station while passengers were trying to board the trains. We decided to focus our search on other forms of transportation as things would not be very different with the long-distance bus stations.

Our initial plan during the beginning of the invasion was to hitch a ride with our neighbour if they decide to evacuate. We discussed the situation with Elena during our daily children's play time with the cats. Elena did not wish to leave her husband alone by himself in Kyiv. And if she were forced to leave, she would rather drive straight into her hometown in Moldova than towards the western regions of Ukraine.

We understood that we could only focus on surviving day to day while getting ready to evacuate at a moment notice. We ate our meals and watched online serials rather calmly as we had become quite emotionally exhausted to even feel gloomy by then.

The nights we spent underground were getting more restless as the intensity of the fight increased, with some of the explosions sounding ever closer. When it was daybreak, we would choose to stay underground as we felt it would be safer to sleep down below than up in our apartment. I think it might be a combination of being drowsy and fearful at the same time, for we tended to fall asleep immediately as the sun rose.

I remember awakening to the sound of a car starting its engine. I got up and saw one of our few remaining neighbours packing carton boxes into his car. I walked over to help him with the loading. He was from Switzerland and could have left days earlier but had lent his car to a friend to evacuate another family. His car had been returned and he decided to leave that morning. He told me he could still squeeze another passenger if I was ready to leave.

I thanked him gratefully and explained that we would not be able to squeeze into his car for I would be leaving together with Natalia and our four cats. We shook hands firmly in silence after loading the last of his boxes into the car and he got in Before driving off, he wound down his window and asked me if I was going to fight.

With a smile, I replied if I had to, I have to.

On the Run

A FEW OF Natalia's friends taking refuge outside Kyiv were becoming hysterical that we were still in the capital as the news was getting increasingly dire. There had been no product replenishments at the supermarket, so the opening hours were shortened to just fours a day.

As we began to consume our stockpile of frozen food, I remember I was thawing out the frozen turkey when I saw the second evacuation notice put out by the Chinese embassy in Kyiv. I presumed that implied that the Chinese foreign service might have obtained confirmation about a sustainable ceasefire, at least long enough for them to organise a second evacuation for their citizens.

There had been many attempts by different representations to negotiate periods of ceasefire for humanitarian corridors. While some ceasefires have been observed, others were blatantly fired upon.

There was no way to know which of those humanitarian corridors might have their ceasefire observed. But it would be rather unlikely for the Russians to fire upon the Chinese evacuation. I was about to share the information with Natalia when she told me that she managed to find a vehicle for us. But we had to leave that very afternoon. I reckoned that our window of opportunity had arrived.

With a rather limited amount of time to complete many tasks, I just dumped everything from the cutting board into the slow cooker and set it to slow cook, subconsciously wondering how many bottles of soya sauce I would need to braise the turkey, Teochew style.

I could not get much information from Natalia as she had a lot of phone calls to make to coordinate our evacuation. The only information I had at that time was that we needed to be by the side of the road with everything packed and ready by four o'clock in the afternoon. Natalia's contacts had found a vehicle for us to drive into Lviv. We did not have any other information regarding the type of vehicle, who our driver was or if anyone else was travelling together with us.

We would need to find a safe place to spend the night as we would not reach Lviv before the start of curfew. We also did not have information on the petrol stations along the way that may still have petrol or diesel for sale. Natalia was trying to find out if any of her friends living along the route would allow us to sleep over for the night with our four cats. I tried to sketch a route map on a paper in case we lose cellular data under any unforeseen circumstances.

Although our getaway bags had already been packed for several days, our electronics and electrical appliances were still scattered all over the place as we had been using them daily. Another issue which we were not prepared for, was what to do with our stockpile of food.

We decided to give the remainder away to our neighbours because food had become quite precious by then. The heaviest things to pack inside the backpack were the two large bags of kitty litter. Because our cats will need to use their toilet while on the road and after they arrive. We had to shave some weight by using the top half of one cat carrier as a makeshift toilet as their regular toilet would not fit into our backpacks.

While I was coiling up all the electrical wires sprawled around our apartment, I recalled reading about how survivors of the second world war had to sew gold ingots into the seams of their clothing before escaping. I mindlessly wondered if anyone had made a crypto wallet in a form of a dental prosthesis.

Natalia finally found a friend living in the city of Vinnytsia about 270 kilometres away that could house us for the night. If we were to drive on the backcountry roads, we should be able to reach our rest stop within four to five hours after one refuelling stop. In theory.

Our neighbours were sad to see us leave when we were sharing our food with them, but everyone was keeping words to the minimum as we bid our farewells and made light jokes about the next potluck session.

Back in our apartment, with our bags placed by the door. Everything was ready except for the cats. We felt it would be better for them to roam about in the common corridor before being confined for hours inside the carriers. Without undoing our shoes, we sat on our doormat and waited patiently for the phone to ring. It could be that the weather was still too cold to be standing by the side of the road or we just wanted to cherish the final moments inside our home.

We were assuming that someone would drive the vehicle to our address and hand the keys over to us, then we would have the time to pack our things properly into the vehicle for the long drive. Natalia received the call that our ride was on its way and that we needed to head downstairs immediately. Gathering our cats into their carriers, we took one last look at our apartment and hoped that nothing would be destroyed before heading down the stairs.

Chitty Chitty Bang Bang

BEING USED TO the surplus of information when using ride hailing app, we tried to contain our anxiety while waiting by the side of the road without a clue about what, where and when our ride was going to appear.

A black-coloured van suddenly turned the corner and stopped right next to us. A stout and bearded driver leaned out from the window to tell us to get in. I glanced over at Natalia to see if she knew who the driver as I was feeling quite unsure. The other guy got out from the passenger seat and opened the rear door of the van. He began loading our backpacks into the van. Still feeling unsure, I went towards the back of the van to help but he gestured for me to get into the van instead.

The van was filled up with boxes right to the roof of the interior. The passenger had to rearrange some of the boxes to make space for the two of us. They managed to free up two seats in the rear for Natalia and I while the cats rested on the armrest between us.

The guys barely said anything to us except that we had to load up and move out quickly as artillery shelling could be

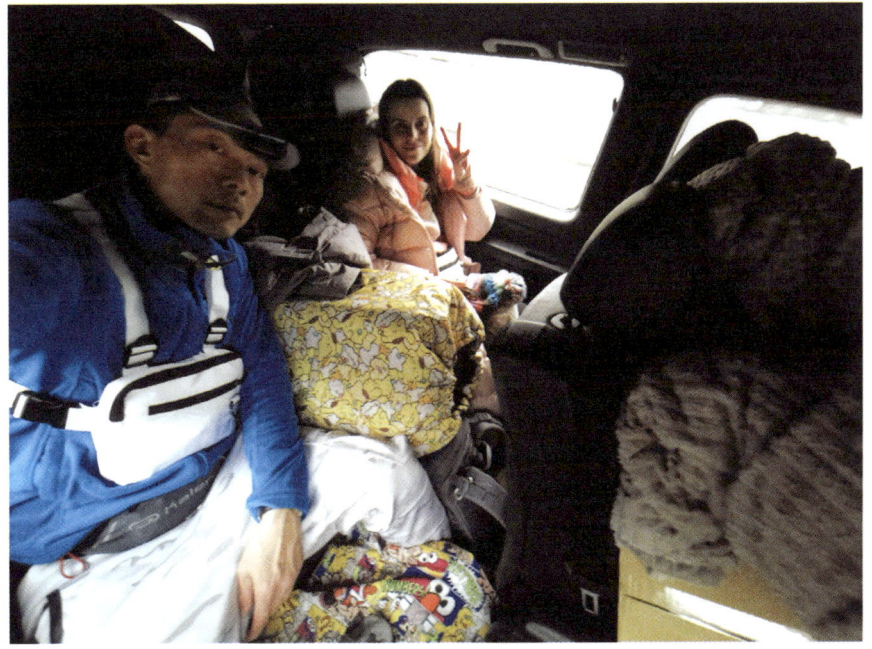

Natalia, the cats and I getting out from Kyiv

heard in the distance. They managed to pack all our belongings into the van and drove off as soon as the doors were shut. Our journey as war refugees had begun.

Looking at how fully packed the van was, I guess we should consider ourselves quite comfortable since we were seated one passenger to a seat. They were carrying so many boxes that I could not help but wonder how they managed to buy all those moving cartons? Because as refugees, we had to pack our belongings into whatever carriers we could get our hands on and were grateful that we did not have to resort to using trash bags. And these guys looked like they were moving house.

The statue of Petro Konashevych-Sahaidachny,
Hetman of Zaporozhian Cossacks

Ukrainian Cossack preparing for war

I could not imagine the luxury of being able to newspaper wrap delicate items before stuffing them into standard-sized moving cartons.

We had just turned into the express way running along the Dnipro River when it suddenly felt like we had crossed into another universe. Maybe it was the first time since we had ventured beyond the supermarket in weeks or the drastic changes to a familiar environment.

We saw the city preparing for war.

The very same road that we used regularly when zipping across town for a restaurant meal had turned into a slow zig-zagging course as we snaked between concrete blocks and iron hedgehogs positioned to slow the advance of any mechanised troops.

Manned by soldiers with rifles and anti-tank weapons, it was reassuring to know that they were Ukrainian but discomforting to be crawling through the bottleneck. Because we could hear the artillery shelling in the background while every vehicle was being funnelled into a congested area.

The driver asked for our passports as we were approaching the end of the zig-zag course. We removed our passports from our pouches as we stopped beside a soldier standing in the middle of the road. Another soldier opened the van doors to inspect the cargo of our van. The driver handed over our passports and presented the documentation for his cargo.

We only discovered by then that he was a member of the militia and was doing a delivery run into the military contested area. All the boxes inside the van were yeast, meant for bakeries that were still trying to operate. Volunteer groups had crowd funded flour and yeast to provide free bread for people who were unable to evacuate from the occupied areas.

The soldiers looked threatening with their balaclavas and weapons when inspecting our van. But I could that see their eyes were smiling when they spotted our cats looking at them curiously from their carriers. They returned our passports after checking and the only question they asked was how many cats we had.

After we cleared our first checkpoint, the guys began to feel more at ease. We started some small talk about the current situation and how crazy the things have become at a rate that was redefining the concept of cope. The car that we were supposed to be driving was parked in an estate about 40 kilometres outside the city. Fortunately, that part of Kyiv was still relatively far away from the fighting.

The plan was to send us into the compound, and we were to drive the car to the owner who was sheltering in Lviv. But the main concern was that petrol stations around the city had stopped selling fuel. We would have to try our luck further away from the city and hope to find a petrol station that may still have fuel to sell.

We drove up to the gates of a beautiful estate and were stopped by security guards with rifles and bullet vests. The guards made a phone call to verify our van registration number before opening the gates to let us through. It was an expensive estate with fancy looking villas scattered among a landscaped forest of pine trees. After about fifteen minutes of driving, we arrived at a rosy-coloured villa. We got out from the van to stretch our legs while the driver tried calling the housekeeper on the phone.

The sky was overcast with a light snowfall drifting down the still air, the place felt serene and idyllic, or it might have been a false sense of safety because the explosions sounded so distant that our instincts were no longer screaming for us to get away.

Moments later, an elderly man emerged and greeted us. I was about to open the rear door of the van to remove our backpacks when the driver told us to get back inside the van. I had already adapted to go with wherever the flow was so I just hopped inside the van and placed the cats carrier on my lap without question. The housekeeper got in the front row and directed us as we continued to wind deeper into the estate.

We finally arrived at the garage building. The owner had more cars than the villa could accommodate so the extra vehicles were parked in another garage. Everyone got out from the van, and I was told that I could transfer our belongings into the car.

Our driver told us that he would be reversing our car onto the driveway from the garage while we unloaded our belongings from the van. Eagerly, I placed the cat carrier on the pavement before opening the rear door of the van. I knew it would be easier to sit on the floorboard of the van for putting on the shoulder straps of my backpack. I was struggling to stand up from the dead weight of my backpack when I heard the roar of the car engine.

IMPRESSIONS OF AN INVASION

Fast and curious – Natalia and Misha

From the deep revving rumble, I knew it had to be some high-performance car. When I finally managed to stand up, I caught a glimpse of our ride reversing into view. It was a Dodge Challenger. Not the same model that US Air Force used for chasing planes but same family nonetheless.

Natalia and I shared a look of disbelief as it was definitely not the make nor model we were expecting. But in situation like that, we could only go with the flow. We placed all our stuff into the car with decent space to spare. After checking that the tire pressures were sufficient, I walked back to the housekeeper to thank him for his help.

By the time I turned around, Natalia had already gotten into the driver seat. I could see how eager she was to drive the car and I doubt her eagerness had much to do with the approaching invaders.

Our driver told us to follow him as he would try to lead us into the country roads. Before getting back into his van, he asked how much fuel there was in the car. Natalia looked at the electronic dashboard with a fancy array, trying to figure out which display indicated the fuel. Our driver walked back towards our car and peered at our dashboard, he pressed some buttons on the steering wheel and shook his head. Our fuel tank was on reserve.

Enough Is Enough

I HAD ANOTHER sudden flashback to my Singapore army days, about an army joke regarding dialect-speaking soldiers colloquially referred to as 'Hokkien Pengs'.

A Hokkien Peng driver was taking his driving test in a three-tonner truck when the tester asks if he was ready for the test.

Hokkien Peng nods enthusiastically.

Tester asks if he had checked the fuel.

Hokkien Peng nods again.

Tester taps at the fuel gauge and asks what the indicator was pointing at.

Hokkien Peng says, "E."

The astonished tester asks what "E" means.

Hokkien Peng replies, "Enough."

Flabbergasted, the tester fumes and asks what "F" means.

Hokkien Peng proudly replies, "Finished."

I felt like I was the tester sitting in the passenger seat wondering if we were finished.

I am not a car enthusiast, so I needed to check the web for specifications relating to our Dodge Challenger. Their engine capacities ranged from 3.6 to 6.2 litres and without the vehicle log card, I was unable to tell what the capacity of our engine was. Our driver clearly anticipated the situation, which was why he had brought a five-litre jerry can in his van. Due to the lack of fuel supply in the city, about a third of the fuel had already been given away to another vehicle.

According to information online, the fuel economy of Challengers range from 13 to 19 miles per gallon. Taking the average in metrics, we could assume a consumption rate about six kilometres per litre of petrol. We needed to mentally prepare ourselves for running out of fuel after passing the 15-kilometre mark. The nearest petrol stations were about two kilometres away, so we decided to head that way. We knew that most petrol stations along the highways were likely to be out of fuel and were not keeping our hopes up.

We drove in silence following the van out of the estate. The jubilation of getting a car to drive out from Kyiv had been dwarfed by the prospect of being stuck in the middle of an invasion in an expensive sports car without fuel. At least our cats were pleasantly intrigued by the smell of the leather seats.

Before entering the highway, we had to merge into a converging car queue at a military checkpoint. The deep rumbling engine of our car growled every now and then as we crawled forward at a torturing pace. I tried to imagine how shipwrecked sailors would have coped if their raft was taking in water faster than they could bail.

We cleared the checkpoint without incident and continued our drive down the highway. The vertical signage of the petrol stations became visible as we curved round a bend but before we got any nearer, we could see the long line of vehicles stretching back several hundred metres along the highway. We did not want to be stuck on the highway as surfaced roads leading into the capital were considered high risk, so we drove past without looking.

I spotted our van driver indicating his intention to filter out from the highway and brought it to Natalia's attention. I could see why she was so focused on the driving because it was helpful to take her mind off things, which could be therapeutic during times like these. I thought that it would be better for her to just focus on the driving while I navigated and worried about all the other crucial variants that we had no control over.

We were greeted shortly by another security checkpoint after exiting from the highway. Although this checkpoint was not manned by soldiers wearing uniforms, I could still see a person pointing the rifle behind the barricade of sandbags. From their age and mismatched camouflage fatigues, my guess was that they were a combination of army reservists and local militia.

Fortunately, not many cars were queuing to pass that checkpoint, so we could cruise toward it without excessive nail-biting movements of the fuel pedal.

The men with rifles eyed our car suspiciously as most decent folks would be speeding down the highway as if running for their lives, literally. The only people not running for their lives would have different intentions, some of which might be questionable.

They checked our passports carefully while another middle-aged man in a black, leather jacket looked through our backpacks and yoga mats. When they understood that we were trying to find a petrol station to refuel, the tension lifted and everyone became very helpful. They obviously knew each other rather well as they began asking among themselves to find out whose neighbourhood still had a petrol station in operation. With no affirmative, they pointed us in the direction of a town which they thought would be most hopeful and waved goodbye to our cats.

We followed our van into the countryside as darkness fell and light discipline was observed everywhere. Without any street lightings, the countryside became pitch black during an overcast night. Most of the cars were driving without the headlights on, and everyone was trying to tailgate the vehicle in front of them with just the illumination from the blinking orange hazard lights. That way, only the first car in the lead needed to turn on the headlights when manoeuvring the bends. Most of the time, just the luminance from the orange blinkers were enough for drivers to make out the lane divider painted in white.

Amazingly, every driver seemed to be able to gauge the width of the road by driving in the middle. Of course, this was possible because the two-lane road had pretty much become a one way route as everybody was trying to leave.

Everyone was driving at a safe speed in order for this unorchestrated dance symphony to perform. It was one of those moments that I realised the illumination from our dashboard was so bright that our reflections on the side windows were restricting what we could see from our sides.

After a period of waltzing down the country road, a quick check on the odometer indicated that we had passed the 15-kilometre mark. And we did not manage to find a petrol station. In fact, none of the roadside shops were open as well. This was one of those times that I sincerely wished I was wrong with my fuel consumption estimations. With no cellular data available, we could not plan for anything, and I could not see any landmarks to help us to locate ourselves.

Our leading van tapped on the brakes before switching off the hazard blinkers. The driver switched on the left indicator light informing us that we should be preparing for a left turn ahead. I could make out the outline of the unlit petrol station against the sky as our vehicles turned into the driveway. Unable to see any lights coming from the fuel pump displays, we were not pinning our hopes that we could refuel our car. We parked our vehicles by the side of the driveway and followed our van driver to knock on the window of the manager office.

Behind the closed blinds, we could see the lights were still on. The manager opened the door slightly and spoke with us. The fuel at the petrol station ran out two days ago. Due to the invasion, fuel allocation had been re-prioritised across the country. He was informed that he might be receiving a delivery the next morning, but they had been telling him about the same thing for the last few days too.

We were somewhere between Kyiv and Vinnytsia with no fuel or hotel, and under freezing temperature. One good thing about our situation was that we did not seem to be near anything of strategic importance that we needed to worry about air-strikes. Or we were just reassuring ourselves of that since it was too dark to see anything anyway.

Our van driver told us that they had to continue with their yeast delivery as it was safer for them to deliver in the dark, and that he would be making some calls to rally for help for our fuel situation. Meanwhile, the safest place thing would be for us to stay inside our car and try to stay as warm as possible. With the curfew starting in the next few hours, we understood that we did not have any choice until the sun rose again. We wished them a safe journey and parted ways with handshakes and hugs.

The petrol station manager was kind enough to let Natalia use the restroom as we prepared ourselves to brave the night. We decided not to use our remaining fuel for heating in case we needed to start the engine to escape whatever distance our fuel could manage. So we huddled together with our cats to share our communal warmth while hoping that the insulation of our car was as good as its fuel appetite.

With the stationary silence, the curiosity of our cats began to override their apprehensions as they began to explore the new surroundings of the car's interior. While they were relieved to get out from their carriers to stretch their legs, Natalia and I were undecided about where to designate their toilet.

Nearly every available space inside a Dodge Challenger was contoured with very little flat spaces. It was not possible to place the toilet basin flatly anywhere without the potential risk of it toppling during use.

We ruled out the option of placing the toilet on the driveway outside the car because the cats may think the reason for throwing them out into the cold exterior was a punishment and not a toilet break.

From my experience of long distances flights with them, I knew they would rather hold their excretions under duress than relieve themselves in an environment without a sense of security. We concluded that the only option was to empty the car trunk of our belongings so we could use the flat area as their toilet.

Putting the torchlight onto my forehead after getting out from the car. I opened the trunk and started removing our belongings and placing them on the driveway. After clearing out the trunk, I managed to open my backpack to retrieve the top half of one of the cargo carriers for the cats. Flipping over the top half to use it as a basin, I opened a bag of cat litter and began pouring a temporary toilet for our cats.

Before I could complete my task, Natalia opened her door and announced that our van driver had managed to find someone to rescue us. Fuel was being sent to our location.

Staring at the unfinished cat toilet and the *pasar malam* goods that I had displayed behind our car, I asked for the estimated time of arrival of our rescuer. Natalia shrugged her shoulders before closing the door to prevent more warm air from escaping. I really had an uncontrollable urge to shout, "*Lelong Lelong.*"

Seize the Night

WE WERE GOING to have to be ready for the refuelling and be back on the road as soon as possible instead of hunkering down for the night. So I had to reverse my previous process to get everything stowed and ready.

After closing the trunk, I decided against waking up the station manager to use the bathroom and guessed it would be easier for me to just walk into one of those bushes by the side of the road. While I was in the mid of watering the plant with biodegradable nutrition, I saw a long convoy of unknown vehicles approaching from afar.

Unable to identify friend or foe in the dark, I began to worry. Not because I did not want to be caught with my fly open but because I would not be able to warn Natalia as the car was parked at a distance away from me. Just like a deer staring into the headlights of an approaching car, I became the human version except that my pee was not caused by fright.

As the convoy got closer, I began to feel less panicked as I could not hear the deep rumbling of heavy mechanised tracks or vehicles. And from the height and position of their headlights, they appeared to be of normal civilian vehicles as well. Feeling rather relieved, I zipped up my pants and walked back normally towards our car.

The lead vehicle of the convoy came to a stop beside me just as I reached the entrance of the driveway to the petrol station. It was an EU plated car with the alphabet 'D', I could see the makeshift label of a red cross on the rear side window of the Volkswagen Touareg when it was at close range. A bespectacled middle-aged man leaned out from the window and asked if the petrol station had any fuel for sale in European-accented English.

For reasons I did not understand, I replied to them in Russian that the station had not been operating for the last two days. They thanked me politely and continued their drive with a puzzled look. I wondered if it was because they did not understand my Russian or it was just the sight of a Chinese man in the middle of nowhere during an invasion of Ukraine. I watched as the convoy of about twenty volunteer vehicles drive by with both admiration and amusement.

Vehicles of all variety were participating in the convoy, from performance off-roaders to soviet era Ladas, family sedans to classic VW beetle. Most were carrying EU license plates, but I had no idea which countries they were from as the alphabets differed from car to car. But everyone had the same determination of braving the risks to deliver help for those who were unable to leave.

I only managed to get back inside the car for some respite from the cold for about fifteen minutes before three vehicles drove into the petrol station in quick succession. They boxed our car in by stopping their vehicles around ours. I guessed that our help had arrived because if they were planning to carjack us, then the six young men would have emerged with weapons drawn.

We came out from our vehicle and introduced ourselves. They were off duty militia from Kyiv who had heard about our situation and volunteered to bring us some fuel. Everyone was anxious and eager to help us with our fuel problem. They opened the tailgate of the pick-up truck and rolled a fuel drum onto the ground. It was a 30-gallon or 113-litre fuel drum, complete with pressure valves for long term storage. I was guessing these guys must have taken it from their fuel depot or somebody really had been prepping for the invasion.

They told us the drum was probably half full but should have enough fuel to get us to the city of Vinnytsia. Someone took out a jackknife and tried to pry open the plug gasket in order to insert a rubber hose for siphoning.

I knew that the jackknife might be able to remove the plug with some luck and difficulty, but sensing everyone enthusiasm, I did not have the heart to point out it was the wrong tool for the job. So I just shone my headlamp and waited politely as another person decided to try his luck with opening the drum after repeated attempts by the first guy. When the third guy suggested we pierce the drum with the knife instead, I told everyone to wait a minute for me.

I dashed back into our car to retrieve my backpack and took out my multi-tool, reconfiguring it into the pliers combination before handing it over to them. They shared a look before taking my multi tool and removed the plug with a lot less effort. Finally, the man who was holding the rubber hose began the process of siphoning fuel.

The height of a 30-gallon fuel drum was about 30 inches or 76 centimetres, while the length of the hose they brought was

1.5 metres. Anyone with siphoning experience will be able tell that this was going to be tricky – with the additional challenge of not being able to place the drum onto the Challenger for fear of damaging the car. I politely suggested that they reverse the pickup against our car and lay the drum on its side.

But one of the things I understood very well was that when youthfulness meets eagerness, it was better to just go with the flow. Valiantly, they replied they would just carry the drum in their arms, it was nothing to worry.

The man holding the hose removed the fuel cap of our car and began to direct the height of the drum as it was held by another two guys in order to stay within the limits of Bernoulli's principle. He placed the hose into his mouth and sucked the fuel out from the drum. As soon as the fuel began to flow, he inserted the hose into our fuel tank, and we started to refuel our car.

There was a little of spillage but that was unavoidable with the procedure. As long as no one was planning to light up a cigarette while we were siphoning, there was nothing to worry about. Our hose man's phone began to ring, and he grabbed it out from his pants pocket to answer the call.

I recalled those warning signs about no handphone usage during refuelling but assumed none of us were worried. Hardly anybody is still using handphones with interchangeable batteries that might have loose contacts these days, and besides, our hose man did not look like a Symbian type of guy.

As our hose man was talking on his phone, the pair of muscled boys holding the drum were beginning to tire from the weight of it. Little by little, the height of the drum began to lower, and just like that. Bernoulli's principle was violated.

Which resulted in an air bubble back flowing into hose disrupting the siphon process completely. It was one of those 'you look at me, I look at you' moments.

They decided to swap guys to support the drum before attempting to siphon again. But since the level of fuel inside the drum had changed, so did the physical equation of siphoning. Making it even tougher with the length of hose we were stuck with. But nothing could deter the perseverance of good teamwork, which these guys had plenty. After some convening and coordination, they managed to position the drum to the appropriate height. Our hose man placed the hose inside his mouth and inhaled deeply.

I had made the similar mistake decades ago, back when I was riding motorcycles. In the nineties, most motorcycles fuel tanks did not have fuel gauges and running out of fuel in the middle of road was not uncommon. Siphoning fuel into or out of containers were a handy skill set to have. But when we suck fuel through the hose by drawing air into our lungs, it takes practice to anticipate the part when the liquid passes the highest point of elevation and then accelerates towards your mouth at an ever-increasing speed.

Our hose man was choked by the surge of the petrol. I felt really sorry for him knowing how badly it stung, for the eyes, nose, mouth and worse of all, the lungs. He began to cough terribly as he dropped the gushing hose while splashing petrol around the car. I lifted up the hose and told the guys to lower the drum. Better to check on our hose man first.

He was leaning over our bonnet red-faced, coughing as hard as he could. With the lungs stinging ever stronger with each cough. I was beginning to worry that he might have induced pulmonary edema. Without a pure oxygen tank there was very little we could do except to let him rest and hope that his breathing returns to normal.

The rest of the guys decided to take turns to continue siphoning but the fuel level had become too low. Fortunately, one of them had brought along a long snot funnel but it did not have a wide mouth. The challenge of pouring a heavy steel drum of petrol into a funnel without a wide mouth was how to control the pour.

Since I was the only one with a headlamp, I suggested that I will hold the funnel while they try to coordinate their effort and control the pour as a team. What began as a delicately-controlled stream deteriorated into wild splashes as the rushing in of air through the same outlet resulted in unpredictable spurts.

Everyone was just hoping for the best while I tried to catch as much of the splattering petrol with the mouth of the funnel. By the time we emptied the fuel drum, we had a small pool of petrol all around us. All we could do was to close the fuel cap and check the gauge while silently hoping that we had enough fuel to reach Vinnytsia.

Natalia started the engine, and everyone waited nervously for her report. She delighted everyone when she announced that our tank was half filled, even our hose man was cheering through his coughs. Natalia and I thanked every one of them gratefully for helping us to get out of our current predicament. They refused to accept any payment for the fuel, repeating that they were there because they volunteered to help. Moved by their benevolence, I shouted, "*Salva Ukraini.*" And like a battle cry, they yelled, "*Heroyam Slava.*"

And just like the balding reservist driver trying his best to deliver ammunition by illegally turning at the bridge near my apartment. I felt fully confident that the defenders of Ukraine would do whatever it took to regain the sovereignty of the country. Perhaps they were a little bit too eager, but there was plenty of undeniable camaraderie.

They told us to follow their cars and that they would lead us onto the motorway connecting to Vinnytsia. Our little convoy started their engines and we tail-gated our lead car into the night.

Still Seizing the Night

I ONLY REALISED that both my hands had a petrol stench when I sat back in the passenger seat. Without water or lather, I will have to make a conscious note to myself not to rub my eyes until I get to wash my hands again.

After driving for about 20 minutes, we saw our lead driver pointing with his left arm as we approached an intersection. We could see a signboard indicating the direction of Vinnystsia and tapped on our horn twice to acknowledge his message. His waved his arm and continued driving straight through the intersection.

It was a stark reminder of civilisation when we turned onto a road with street lighting. Not those tangerine-coloured sodium vapour ones that are found in cities but white-coloured mercury vapour street lamps from another generation. The street lamps accompanied us for a short section of the drive before disappearing from the rear-view mirror, I guessed that intersection was far away enough from Kyiv to remained safely lit. We took the chance of switching on our headlights in low beam mode for driving on a dark lonely road. With no cars in front or behind us, it then occurred to me that we were truly on our own.

With cellular network coverage, we managed to locate our position and could even provide an estimated time of arrival for our destination. Natalia called our host and informed him of our latest development. Without any further inconvenience, we should be arriving slightly after midnight.

Natalia had to slam the brakes suddenly when our headlights illuminated a pile of concrete blocks in the middle of the road. Only then did we realise how stressful being the lead driver of a convoy must have been when driving through unlit roads. Because unlike peace time roadworks that placed warning blinkers at spaced out intervals. Security roadblocks are meant to catch the drivers unaware. We rounded the concrete blocks slowly and zig-zagged towards a group of armed soldiers waving us forward.

We wound down our windows before coming to a complete stop. With no other cars in front or behind us, we had the undivided attention of everyone manning the checkpoint. The soldier told us to switch off our engine and turn off the headlights while keeping the interior lights on. We complied with his instructions and handed over our passports without question. He shone a torchlight at our documents while another soldier shone his into the interiors while walking around the car.

After looking through our passports, he asked where we were heading. Natalia replied that we were on our way to Vinnystsia. He leaned lower to study our faces before asking why we were travelling during the hours of a curfew. Natalia explained the short version of our fuel situation. He then asked about the contents we were carrying inside our car. Natalia answered it was the belongings we took when we fled Kyiv with our four cats. He asked whether the cats were from Ukraine or Singapore. We giggled before replying that they were actually from China.

He returned our passports and explained the procedure we had abide by when approaching military checkpoints during curfew hours, we had to be very careful because all security personnel were authorised to shoot.

Natalia thanked him by valiantly shouting *Slava Ukraini*. But instead of responding with a *Heroyam Slava*, he looked at me and waited. Natalia turned to me and pumped her fist while saying *Slava Ukraini*. At that moment I was not fully aware what response were expected of me, so I just nodded my head. Natalia repeated *Slava Ukraini* with even more gusto while looking at me expectantly.

From my encounter with the militia boys who had helped us earlier, I felt it would not be adequate for me to reply *Heroyam Salva* in front of uniformed personnel because I was not a Ukrainian. Getting impatient, Natalia repeated *Slava Ukraini* while glaring at me. Not feeling very confident, I replied, "*Boodmore, Boodmore, Boodmore.*"

Natalia hung down her head in embarrassment while the soldier bended backwards laughing towards the sky. He tapped on the top of our car to wave us on our way before walking towards the other soldier behind the machine gun to share the funny moment.

There are only a few Ukrainian words I had in my vocabulary, and one of them is *Boodmore*. The Slavic drinking culture is rather complex – what we generically use as 'cheers' while clinking glasses would be viewed as shallow if toasting to a person of stature or to a higher clause. In the Russian language, there are about forty different types of toasts to use at different occasions and with different people. Likewise, the Ukrainian language had its own variants. *'Boodmore'* actually means 'let us be'. Embracing the free spirit of Cossacks riding into battle with a grin, *Boodmore* has become the toast among Ukrainians that means a lot more than just 'cheers'. I suppose that during the period of martial law when alcohol sale was banned, what I said might have created more reminiscence than just humour for those soldiers at the checkpoint.

We continued to drive with very little traffic and a very helpful GPS navigation provided by the cellular networks, switching between providers freely without any interruptions as inter-rivalries between the telecommunication companies had dissipated with a click of the mouse.

There were several more checkpoints along the journey, but we navigated each of those smoothly by following the procedure ardently. But one of the checkpoints was quite memorable because it was manned by a group of men who were quite advanced in age. I believed it could have been a gathering of grandfathers, and I swear two of them looked like Santa Claus in tactical gear. What made their checkpoint stand out was that they were giving out stalks of flower to every female driver or passenger that passed through. Because it was past midnight by the time we went across their checkpoint, the date became 8th March.

IMPRESSIONS OF AN INVASION

International Women's Day is a big deal in Ukraine. Regardless of the rocket attacks, bomb explosions or flying bullets, a military invasion is no excuse to ignore the importance of women in our lives. As long as the sun makes flowers bloom, women will be honoured. Natalia was delightfully cheered by the gift of a single flower after all that we had been through. I was just convinced that they must have been Santa Claus-es in camo.

We cleared one last checkpoint before entering the city boundary of Vinnystsia. Rows of bright street lamps and urban architecture ushered a soothing sense of safety, affirming that we had left the frontline.

We were driving toward the home of our host when I spotted a petrol station with a brightly lit signboard across the road. They were even displaying the different prices for different types of fuel that were available. Having experienced fuel shortage like we did, it was understandable how we were jumping in our seats excitingly while turning the car around to drive towards the petrol station.

When we asked the pump attendant if there were any fuel for sale at that hour, he assured us smilingly that we could not get luckier with our timing. They were just resupplied a few hours ago and had just finished filling up all the cars that were queuing since the afternoon. The icing on the cake was that they also had the 92 octane level fuel that could enhance our engine performance. Believing that it must have been lady's luck on Women's Day, we filled up our tank until the attendant insisted that it could not be filled any more.

Having Seized the Night

BY THE TIME we reached our host apartment, it was already past 1AM in the morning. The roads were easy to navigate as there was very light traffic. But trying to find the apartment when every other building was observing light discipline was a bit tricky because the block numbers were not illuminated. All the buildings looked like one adjoining structure clumped together.

Our host was telling us that the entrance to his apartment was next to a restaurant. The challenge for us was trying to read those unlit signboards of different restaurants around his neighbourhood in the dark. After finding the correct building, we needed a safe place to park car for the night. During times of turmoil, hardly anyone would park their cars along the street. We were told that there was one enclosed carpark across the street with proper security, we just needed to pay the overnight parking fee and the car would be safe.

We had to wake the carpark security guard from his office and wait for him to put on his winter jacket. After that, he needed to walk across the carpark to open the steel gates for us to drive through. He was very understanding and guided us to a parking lot as the snow became heavier.

IMPRESSIONS OF AN INVASION

Perhaps it was our first time as refugees or fatigue from our adventure, we ended up waking the security guard two more times to repeat this process of changing from pyjamas and slippers to winter jacket and boots, traversing across the carpark in the snow, opening and locking the steel gates for us. During our first trip into our host apartment, we only brought our cats and backpacks but forgot the half-prepared cat toilet inside the trunk. So a second trip for the cat litter was required. But since the apartment was already overcrowded, the only place we could sleep was on the floor, so had to return to the car for the third time because we needed our yoga mats which were stuffed under the car seats.

Our host had moved to Vinnystsia with his wife and two daughters from Kyiv during the early part of the invasion. As the situation deteriorated, his mother left her hometown in eastern Ukraine and joined them. Later on, fearing for the safety of his ex-wife and son. He requested that his ex-wife and son be moved into the apartment with his ex-mother-in-law in tow. We had become the refugee couple with four cats crashing in with their multi-tiered family all under one roof.

The children were excited to see our cats as we woke everyone up with our arrival. Our host's wife made us a supper of dumplings and soup, and we were very grateful for the hot meal. We understood that the mood of the city was not dire even though there had been a missile attack on their airport a week ago.

Everyone was confident that Kyiv will not fall but it was not possible to predict how much destruction the invaders would be inflicting on the city during the siege.

We were advised to resume our journey the moment the curfew was lifted because the flow of exodus traffic will be getting heavier by the hour. Any traffic accident might create miles of vehicle pile-ups, which may be a death trap for anyone who is stuck within the stretch.

After supper, we unrolled our yoga mats and collapsed onto their living room floor.

Road Tripping

WE ROSE BEFORE the sun due to our cats playing around in a new environment – our dominant female was even bold enough to challenge their dog.

While we were freshening up, our host's mother was kind enough to prepare a wholesome breakfast for us. Food might have diminished in terms of variety, but the quantity did not suffer. A hearty breakfast of toast with bacon and eggs, complimented with pancakes and jam, was more than we could have asked for. We bid our heartfelt goodbyes to our hosts with everyone hoping for a more joyous gathering back at Kyiv when the opportunity arises.

We carried all our belongings back to our car in a single trip and were planning to give the carpark security guard a tip for troubling him the night before. He outrightly refused for he believed it wasn't right to help refugees for monetary benefit, he gave us our change for the parking fee and wished us Godspeed as he sincerely believed we were going to need it.

As the engine was warming up, we discussed who ought to be doing the driving, for Lviv was about 400 kilometres away. Natalia felt that she was more energetic in the morning so she preferred that I take over the driving after our first pit stop.

We cruised out of the residential neighbourhood by navigating our GPS. The weather was supposed to be good for

Aghast and curious – Misha looking out for danger

driving as it was a cloudy day with bright sunshine. Heading for the highway connecting Vinnystsia to Lviv, we blended into the morning traffic of the city.

Vinnystsia looked just like any other city waking up to a lovely morning except for the missing presence of school-going children, along with the appearance of sandbag-fortified checkpoints at major intersections. After curfew was lifted, most cars carrying women and children were seen weaving through the checkpoints.

IMPRESSIONS OF AN INVASION

There were a lot of vehicles heading in the westerly direction and once we got on the highway, we joined the steady flow of vehicles heading west. Few cars were driving in the opposite direction. Many cars carried Kyiv registration plates but we saw several cars from the eastern regions as well. Almost every car had stuck an A4-sized paper displaying the word дети, meaning 'children' in Russian. I was in awe of the mindset of those risk-taking drivers while as we were constantly overtaken by their speeding cars.

Maybe the presence of children created a stronger sense of urgency, or it could have been a speed demon pretending to carry children onboard. We concluded that we should just drive at the optimum speed for fuel efficiency.

Our fuel tank was still three quarters full when we started in the morning. Estimating with a large margin for error, I believed that we would be able to cover 480 kilometres without any unforeseen circumstances. But having learnt the lesson of running out of fuel, we decided there would be no harm in preparing ourselves for those unforeseen circumstances as well. With that in mind, I suggested that we stay our course until we pass the half-tank mark. After that, we should refuel anywhere along the way and swap drivers.

With Natalia behind the wheel, I began to check for updates about the latest developments in Ukraine. We found out that the exclusive estate where our car had been garaged was struck by rockets last night. We hoped that everyone had survived the air strike by remaining inside their bunkers.

The Homostel airport which was about 10 kilometres outside of Kyiv experienced nonstop fighting, the airport had been changing hands between invaders and defenders so frequently that it was difficult to tell new information from the old. The Russians had been trying to reach Kyiv after establishing a bridgehead at the airport. But fierce and creative resistance by Ukrainian defenders in the surrounding areas had denied the invaders of much territorial gains. As long as the Ukrainian brigade in city of Chernihiv was stopping the North-eastern onslaught by numerous Russian battle groups, the encirclement of Kyiv would not be possible. We saw so many reports of the invaders being destroyed by the Chernihiv defenders repeatedly that I was beginning to wonder if the Ukrainians were trying to repeat the same story so that its people would not lose hope.

Our next-door neighbour was beginning to miss us, and our departure incited her to contemplate her own evacuation as well. As for Natalia's mother and grandma in Odesa, there were constant missile attacks around the port due to the guided missile cruiser Moskva loitering near their horizon. They were relieved to know that we had gotten out of the capital and were praying for our safety.

By late morning, traffic on the highway had gotten heavier as the number of cars gradually increased. A quick check on our GPS highlighted our route flashing in red and showed a few alternative suggestions. I shared the traffic update with Natalia and we decided that mobility was fundamental and we had to avoid congestion at all cost.

I chose an alternative route with the lightest traffic but with an additional distance of 20 kilometres. But it was still within our fuel limitations. We turned out from the highway on the next exit and began heading north instead of west.

IMPRESSIONS OF AN INVASION

This massive traffic exodus was a true test for the integration of info-communications with the transportation system. While the eastern, southern and capital of Ukraine were busy fighting their respective battles, the west had to shoulder the responsibility of resupplying resources to the various fronts, and coordinate the exodus of millions of refugees at the same time.

Traffic police from different cities in the western region were out in full force to help with accidents or blockages, and roads were diverted or rerouted to ensure the continuity of the traffic flow regardless of the surge in volume and endless air raid alerts. The efforts by the network of traffic police were uploaded almost in real time to the national road traffic website, which were in turn relayed to every navigational app in use. We really appreciated the contribution from everyone chipping in to help with the evacuation of refugees. From the pensioners volunteering to direct traffic in the cold to system engineers ensuring the operability of information technology.

After another detour, our tank was half full. We proceeded according to plan by looking out for suitable petrol stations to refuel along the way. The petrol stations situated along the highways were usually constructed as rest stops with food, toilets and convenience stores, which attract drivers to them like bees to honey in times of fuel emergencies.

The first petrol station we spotted was not from the vertical signboard but from the horizontal queue of cars that had lined up kilometres before the petrol station. Natalia did not even bother to slow down and we just drove past all the waiting cars. Only after passing the petrol station did we see from the fuel prices on display that only diesel was available.

We had passed our half-tank mark with only half the distance covered, which placed us in a precarious position. I suggested in the event we were unable to refuel, we could park the car in a petrol station after reaching the outskirts of Lviv, just in case we had to wait for the empty petrol station to be resupplied. But if we were to run out of fuel inside Lviv city before reaching the apartment, then it would be like stumbling near the finish line.

Natalia told me to come up with a plan because she needed to concentrate on the driving, which was on a rather straight highway.

Taking a quick look at the map, the nearest city with several intersecting highways was Ternopil. I was taking a blind bet that any well-connected city would be able to maintain a decent supply of fuel even through those times. But we would only be able to find out if we filtered out of the highway to drive into the city.

I quickly found a street inside Ternopil with several petrol stations displaying the word 'Open' in the app and selected a new route toward that street. Natalia did not bother asking why when I told her to turn out of the highway at the upcoming exit.

Pit Stop

IT WAS A nice change of scenery from the endless stretch of highway when we were greeted by the urban landscape of Ternopil.

We have a friend living inside the city but decided against meeting up with him as it likely meant spending the night in Ternopil. It would be rude to do a quick 'hi and bye' considering our friendship. But it would be mischievously acceptable to send a video of us circling the Ternopil roundabout as we enter the city to him instead.

When we arrived at that street on the app with several opened petrol stations, we discovered the meaning of 'open' was in reference to the convenience stores. The availability of fuel was still dire – out of the several petrol stations, only one had diesel to sell. Even international conglomerates like Shell only had empty dashes to display on their price board. We decided to stop at one of the petrol stations to hatch another plan.

I was baffled that even international brands like Shell had run out of fuel. In that case, which company would have access to strategic fuel storages? I asked Natalia if she could recall the brand of the petrol we used to refuel our car the night before. Apparently, they are the market leader in Ukraine with their own tank farms. I immediately searched for their nearest petrol station, which was about 10 kilometres away.

We found the petrol station after about twenty minutes of driving. Just like the night before, their price board displayed availability of every type of fuel. Fortunately, the car queue was only several hundred metres long. We just needed to find a suitable junction to make a U-turn and line up behind the waiting cars.

I saw a turn off slightly beyond the car queue and alerted Natalia to it, she flicked on the directional indicators and slowed down before turning into a small street. We then turned the car into a two-lane street that led to a gated compound. Standing in front of the closed gates were fully armed soldiers wondering why a Dodge Challenger had turned into the entrance of their military base.

We smiled politely at the onlooking soldiers as Natalia attempted to perform a three-point turn with the manual steering of the car. Finally, one soldier approached our car and asked what we were up to. Natalia explained that we were planning to use the two-lane entrance of their military base to turn our car so that we could join the line of cars queuing up for fuel. He nodded understandingly and helped to guide Natalia with the turning radius so that the side skirts of the Challenger would not be scratched by the pavement. We turned our car successfully and finally joined the line of cars waiting by the side of the road leading towards the fuel station.

I told Natalia that I saw fresh bananas on display in the row of shops not far from the petrol station and suggested she waited in line with the rest of the drivers while I search for lunch. I got out from the car and began walking back in the direction that we had driven.

IMPRESSIONS OF AN INVASION

Along the way, I saw a lot of soldiers standing by chatting amongst themselves. I assumed the military base might be a mobilisation centre as most of the soldiers were middle-aged men wearing ill-fitting uniforms. Many of them were probably also wondering who the Chinese guy walking next to their military base was. I suddenly realised that I had better prepare to be questioned as a stranger coming into their town.

I entered the first grocery store that I came across. It was a well-stocked little shop with plenty of meats, cheeses and sausages. I wanted something that we could easily eat on the road, so I bought some smoked meat, bread, oranges and bananas, swinging my plastic bag of groceries with the bananas while walking back toward the petrol station. I assumed that the soldiers no longer felt that this Chinese looked overly suspicious.

By the time I returned to Natalia, she had already moved our car inside the petrol station. We only had to wait for a few more cars before it was our turn to refuel. I got into the car and showed her the oranges and bananas I had found. It was revitalising to finally have access to fresh fruits and fuel again.

An elderly man was refuelling his old soviet ZAZ car in front of us. After refueling, he reached into his car and placed two fuel cans next to the pump. I was a little taken back as those cans appeared to be just as old as the car. That old man was clearly prepared for times like this. Natalia explained that anyone who had endured the years before and after the collapse of the USSR were unlikely to ever be caught unprepared again.

When it was our turn at the fuel pump, we filled up our tank to the maximum even though we knew that Lviv was only about a hundred kilometres away.

After refuelling, Natalia drove into a parking lot inside the petrol station and suggested it was time for us to switch drivers after her toilet break. After adjusting the height and position of the driver seat for myself, I decided it would be more practical to make the sandwiches before moving off. Firstly, I could eat them while driving. Secondly, it would be safer for us to be slicing the chunk of smoked meat while the car was not moving.

Natalia started with the fruits while I prepared our open-faced sandwiches. In fact, we were so hungry and happy that we ended up having a small picnic inside the petrol station instead.

Fuel at last – like bees swarming towards a pot of honey

IMPRESSIONS OF AN INVASION

It was not long before our cats began fidgeting from the stationary silence and the scent of our food. Natalia suggested that we might as well let them out for a toilet break. We had eaten, our fuel tank was full, and we were still early on our schedule. I nodded in agreement and opened the car door.

The spellbinding shrills of an air raid siren suddenly pierced through the air.

I turned to see Natalia staring at me with a half-eaten sandwich just as a cat was climbing onto her lap. Instinctively, we wanted to dash for the nearest underground shelter. But we were likely just above the fuel reservoir of the petrol station, not an ideal bunker to squeeze into.

Shutting the door, I started the engine while trying to reach for my seat belt. All the cars that had congregated around the petrol station were disappearing fast. I saw the pump attendant running away after hitting the emergency stop switch.

I reversed our car from the parking lot and sped out of the petrol station. We could still hear the air raid sirens even with our windows closed and engine running. Without any underground carpark to drive into, I assumed the safest place while driving with open skies above our head would be to get away from the urbanised and industrial area that we were in.

I remembered the nearest way to join the highway was to the south of us, so I made a right turn at the next junction in the direction of the highway. But navigating in urban roads was very different from rural motorways, we found ourselves stuck among cars waiting for the traffic lights to change as everyone was headed to the same highway.

IX SHEN

Cars scattering away as sirens blasted

The wailing of the sirens was relentless while we waited motionless with all the cars trapped by the red-coloured traffic lights. We were surrounded by industrial buildings with a network of electrical transmission towers criss-crossing above us.

Natalia was clearly upset that I had driven us into a death-trap. I asked her to help with the navigation by searching for any alternative route to access the motorways. It could have been the stress from the air raid sirens, the sense of helplessness being stuck in traffic or the frustration of an unfinished sandwich. But I guess that there might be some truth to the myth about women and maps.

By the time our traffic lights turned green, Natalia still could not find an alternative route even though the ranting had never stopped. So I turned into another road where the traffic was at least moving to avoid being stuck at the next traffic light down the same road.

When everyone is heading for the same exit of a collapsing tunnel, no matter how orderly things were, I reckon the odds of hiding among the rubble would be the same as those at the end of the line.

Driving along the road where traffic was still flowing, we ended up back on the road between the petrol station and military base again. It was quite exciting to be driving between them with the air raid sirens blasting around us.

The soldiers were nowhere to be seen as I assumed they would have bunkers to run into while the petrol station had become completely deserted.

Instead of making a dash for the highway with all those cars in panic, my plan was to find a safer place inside the city where we could wait for the mad rush to subside. I was racing through my mind trying to remember all the landmarks that we drove past earlier.

I recalled the large roundabout where I made a video. I guessed it might be safe if we could drive onto the middle of it. Or the opposite might be true if the Kremlin intended to make a statement by targeting a landmark in the city. In chronological order, the next landmark I recalled was a reservoir which I thought would make a nice picnic spot. With the open space and unobstructed views, I was hoping that it would be an unlikely target for an air raid. I immediately down-shifted the gear for more torque and did a fast but not furious sprint towards that picnic spot I was fixated on in my mind.

The traffic was rather light during an air raid, allowing me to swerve precariously through the winding road toward the reservoir. After stopping under a tree with a relatively decent view of the reservoir, I explained to Natalia that I believed it would be safest for us to remain in our position until the air raid was over.

I was hoping that the serenity of the place could help to clam her down as we continued with our picnic which had been so rudely interrupted.

The Last Stretch

BY THE TIME our cats returned into their carriers after emptying their bowels, the air raid had ended for more than half an hour. Natalia claimed that she would prefer to drive because she felt that I had been rather reckless when we were racing towards the picnic spot with way too much adrenaline. Besides, I was also the better navigator between the two of us.

I was hoping that she would get a break from driving all day before but since she had become fully alert after our missile scare, I just swapped places with her without any fuss.

Picking a route towards Lviv, we fastened our seat belts and started the engine. We cruised along the countryside after leaving Ternopil with a scenic drive in the direction of the setting sun, it would have been a lovely holiday moment if we were not refugees on the run by valeting someone else's car.

Somewhere between Ternopil and Lviv, a volunteer traffic controller in a neon orange vest was directing the cars from the motorway onto a smaller road. We stopped our car beside him to ask why we needed to detour as the motorway was leading directly towards Lviv. He explained that every car on that road was also heading to Lviv as well, and that we just had to follow the other cars in front of us as they had set up traffic marshals to direct everyone.

We turned off the motorway and drove onto a dusty track with thick bushes and low trees. I turned around to see all the cars following us, I thought we should be safe as long as everyone was travelling together. Unless this was a well-organised car-jacking operation on a scale we had not imagined, we should have nothing to worry about.

At the end of the dusty track was another volunteer directing traffic onto a narrow asphalt road. When we saw some small houses dotted along the narrow road, our minds began to feel at ease, knowing that we had not been diverted into some discreet and quiet place.

We were twisting and turning through the narrow countryside road with the directions given to us from volunteers located at different junctions. We even saw a gathering of ladies with head scarves at one junction chatting among themselves while looking at all the cars from other cities driving through their neighbourhood.

They must be in as much wonder as us about what was going on. We finally turned onto a wider road where all the cars were piled up into four lanes, using up two of the lanes meant for the opposite direction. It was a cross junction without any traffic lights but there were a few policemen in tactical gear controlling the situation.

And just like a railway crossing, we witnessed a convoy of tanks being transported on trailers. Most of the tanks had varying degree of damage, a few had the letter 'Z' on them while other did not. We had been diverted away from the motorway to give way for the transportation of those tanks.

I guessed those tanks were being sent to the repair facilities in the western region of Ukraine. Many of the cars waiting at the junction were tweeting their horns in jubilation of seeing damaged Russian tanks. I did not know the length of the convoy but I counted at least three tanks passing us before the cars began moving.

We continued to cruise along the countryside road until we came across a small town – one of those that sprouted out on both sides of the road that cut across it. I spotted some open post offices and shops, and told Natalia to stop the car by the side of the road. I got out and crossed the road quickly, making a beeline for the row of sellers displaying colourful fresh produce.

After having our run in with the grandfathers garrison last night, I was reminded that it was Women Day that day. The town folks had set up temporary tables selling flowers along the road. I presumed those flowers were from the local nurseries as they were mostly of the same variety.

I was trying to seize the opportunity to buy fresh flowers for Natalia on 8th March while on the run from a military invasion, as it would be a sin on mankind if I did not pick up that perk-me-up for her.

We were enjoying our sunset drive into the outskirts of Lviv when Natalia tried contacting our friend inside the city. He was glad that we managed to get out from Kyiv and really looked forward to meeting us in Lviv. Unfortunately, due to the huge influx of people rushing into Lviv, there was a dire shortage of housing available.

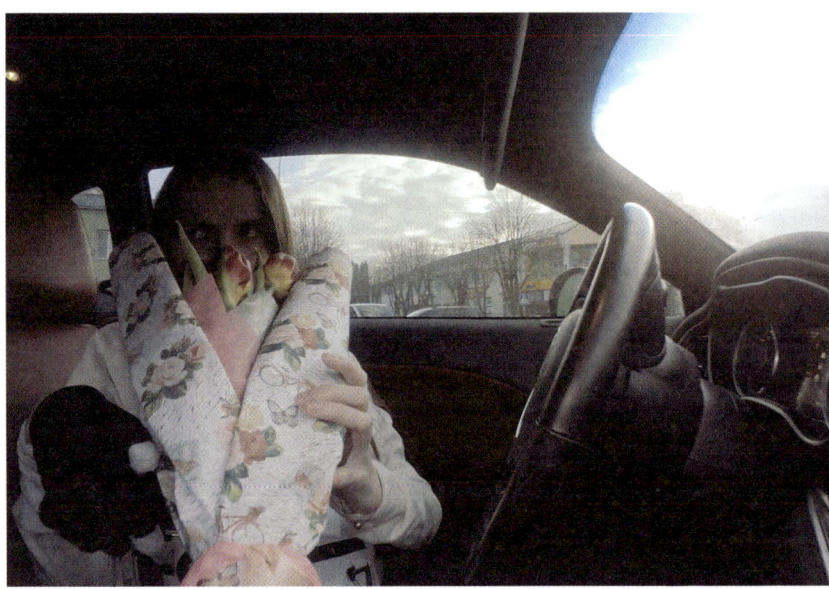

Left: **Prevailing flowers in peace or war**

Bottom left: **Fresh flowers from an old romantic**

Bottom right: **Flower from an even older romantic**

Escaping from the storm

Driving into the sunset

The situation was so desperate that some of reservations were refunded because refugees were being served on a 'first come, first serve' basis. So the flat that he mentioned earlier had already been rented out to a family of five who arrived before us. He suggested we crash on the sofa at the apartment he shared with a flatmate until an available place popped up or consider squeezing into the community shelters provided by the city.

Lviv is a tourist-friendly city with plenty of accommodation for visitors in normal times. But when everyone was thinking alike during abnormal times, we ended up becoming just like one of those koi fish in a congested pond, vying for one popular feeding spot.

We were so focused on reaching Lviv that we overlooked securing our accommodations. Although we were mentally prepared to sleep on the streets as refugees if we had to, the dread of not knowing how long we would be needing to sleep on the streets was most daunting. I opened up all the accommodation booking apps available on my phone and began searching desperately while Natalia kept her eyes on the road as the sky darkened.

I believe many well-intentioned people wanted to help Ukrainians with the country situation. Some of those helpful people wanted to support the Ukrainians by donating money directly to the people instead of through organisations. They came up with the idea of booking and paying for accommodations online while leaving it empty at the discretion of the landlord to let any refugees in at the owner's choosing.

It was a gracious gesture that went viral. But it also unleashed all the problems that a reservations management software had been designed to solve, that resulted in people like us being unable to find any available accommodation while many places were also fully paid and left vacant.

Because there was no more high tech means of pairing homeless people with available accommodation, matching arriving refugees with suitable housing became a chaotic task. Every online accommodation in the Lviv was booked and there was nothing available to rent for the next few months. We had to solve the problem the old fashioned way – by calling up as many owners as we could find. Natalia and I swapped places so she could start contacting as many owners as she could in hopes of finding a unit while I navigated our way into the city.

The tricky thing about driving is that one needs to have a destination in order to drive. I was clueless as to where we should be heading as we joined the flow of cars entering into the city.

To think that we had left our comfortable and well stocked apartment in Kyiv so that we could make a mad dash across the country, only to end up sleeping on park benches was a thought too negative to be spiralling into.

And just like the Frogger arcade game, we were drifting amid the flow of cars without any suitable spot to leap onto. We were more or less driving in eccentric circles like the frogger, when one home owner finally replied to Natalia out of the countless others she had messaged. The owner was actually being polite by calling her to reject our request because his property was not pet-friendly.

Natalia was probably at the end of her emotional straw at that moment because she broke down in tears and sobbingly pleaded for the owner to make an exception for us. She earnestly assured him that we were willing to take full responsibility of any potential damages as long as he lets us stay.

We inevitably ended up having to use the refugee card to find a place to stay but I believed we had earned our right by then. After a conscience searching delay, the owner agreed to our request.

Soft Beds Are Hard to Sleep

AFTER WEEKS OF sleeping fully attired on hard floors in readiness to run, the bounce of the mattress's springs as I laid down in pyjamas felt too foreign.

Looking at the shadows from a tree being cast onto the walls by street lamps that did not need to be turned off, my mind scrambled, searching for input from every sensory system. The photo receptors in my retinas were firing in overdrive and my entire body was warning that something was very unusual about my current environment.

It was quiet and comfortable.

It did not really matter whether it was neuro-psychological or behavioural neurology, I did not have the luxury to intrigue myself as we were not yet out of the woods. The owner of the flat was only willing to let us stay for two nights, so the countdown to our homelessness was like the trickling sands of a 48-hour sand dial.

Early the next day, while roaming the city in search of available flats, we passed by a community shelter. It was a brutal sight to watch fleeing people. Refugees of all ages were coming and leaving through the entrance gates piled up high with sandbags. Volunteers were assisting and directing as food and clothes were distributed, some of the refugees had to flee their homes with no time to pack.

Unlike makeshift dormitories during the COVID isolation craze, shelters had to serve as bomb shelters during an invasion. Most of these shelters were underground storages that were hastily converted into housing for people seeking safety during an air raid. It was definitely not meant for people hoping to stay for any extended period of time. If we do not manage to secure available accommodation, leaving Lviv might be the more viable option.

We met up with our friend in the city centre after returning the Dodge Challenger to the owner. It was also our first restaurant meal since the outbreak of the invasion. Sitting at our chequered cloth table with bustling waitresses and dining music, I was wondering why we were not freaking out. Maybe because many of the diners were dining in bullet vests while carrying firearms. Eating inside a pizza restaurant with so many people preparing for war, it felt like we were in a Mafia movie, except that no one was speaking Italian.

Our friend was telling us about the insane increase in rental prices as demand had outstripped the available supply. He explained that it will be more challenging for us, since we were competing against refugees with larger families consisting of multiple members for a single flat.

It was quite common for three-bedroom flats to house three or more families. Which made me think of the early Chinese immigrants in Singapore living in their five-foot-way quarters before the availability of public housing.

IMPRESSIONS OF AN INVASION

Lviv – apartments everywhere but no abode

Natalia managed to find a friend who was willing to host us at his workers dormitory next to his factory in the city of Ivano-Frankivsk. But getting there would be another transportation challenge and the idea of staying in a factory during the air raids was not very appealing. We looked at the availability of farmhouses in the remote regions of the western regions, but even those were full. It seemed like everyone felt that the rural areas were less dangerous than the urban ones. But we had friends that recounted seeing Russian tanks busting through the woods around their village. No place could be deemed safe as long as the invasion was ongoing.

After we finished our desserts, our friend earnestly suggested that we consider the idea of crossing the border into Poland. Poland was a NATO member and could offer us a better sense of security. At the very least, we would not have to live under constant air raid alerts. Although there was also an overcrowding of refugees in the city of Warsaw, many other Polish cities and towns still had available accommodation to offer. He felt that we would have better luck trying to find a place to stay in a Polish city or town.

We knew of several ways to cross the border but needed to get the necessary vaccinations for our cats in order to enter the European Union. We hoped that the veterinarian clinics in Lviv were operating as normal despite the constant threat of air strikes. Fortunately, we managed to find a clinic that could provide all the necessary procedures for pets entering into the European Union.

Unfortunately though, like any operating businesses being overwhelmed, they had no available appointment for weeks. But acknowledging that we were being responsible pet owners in times of turmoil, she told us that we could camp with our cats at the clinic tomorrow and try our luck in between slots.

We needed more time in Lviv to plan our next course of action. Extending our stay meant that we would face the possibility of homelessness on our third night in Lviv. Natalia had to plead with the flat owner for an extension of two more nights so that we could make all the necessary arrangements for our departure. To our surprise, the owner agreed without fuss. Apparently it was a common situation, with many of the refugees transiting through the city.

The mayhem of getting oriented upon arrival and the sudden preparation for another departure in the midst of an invasion was like trying to pour *teh tarik* on a swing. We heard of people waiting overnight on the platforms of the train stations in freezing temperatures just to squeeze onto trains.

Even though there were many additional freight trains travelling to newly assigned cities helping to receive refugees in Europe. The availability of train wagons, undestroyed railway tracks and rail traffic coordination within Europe made the scheduling of these trains a mammoth masterclass in crisis management.

Having learnt our lesson about securing accommodation while on the run, we decided it would be wiser for us to confirm our next accommodation before joining the exodus bandwagon. Warsaw has a good transportation network connecting it with Ukraine. Unavoidably, it became the Polish city to receive the highest number of Ukrainian refugees.

We started searching online for flats that we could rent for a few months. Some of our friends had found places to live in Warsaw and informed us that the influx of people seeking accommodation in Warsaw was just like in Lviv. Although many friends were willing to house us temporarily until we find a place for ourselves, the squeeze on the Warsaw rental market was unlikely to change as long as the fighting remained intense in Ukraine.

Many refugees had chosen to move into other cities after a period of unsuccessful attempts at finding suitable housing, or they just did not want to live communally inside those community shelters any longer than they had to.

The perks of planning an evacuation from Lviv was that we could do it inside a nice café while people watching. Unlike Kyiv, listening to jazz music instead of multiple explosions really made decision making a lot more less stressful.

We knew that there were plenty of international volunteer groups in Warsaw helping to sort out the arriving refugees into different cities scattered around Europe. But different cities had different criteria with the way housing was allocated. We had friends that were sent to Italy, Germany and Sweden. But none of them knew where they were going until they roamed through the maze of volunteer tents set up like a carnival attracting refugees to move into their cities. It came down to luck regarding the type of accommodation or location you end up in.

We expanded our scope beyond Warsaw and included a few other cities in our shortlist – Katowice, Krakow and Gdansk. Katowice has very good transportation network, which would be essential if we needed to escape from further escalation, should Kremlin enlarge the scale of its military conflict. Krakow has a lot of accommodation as a city for tourism. Gdansk has access to sea routes in the event of extreme evacuation but its proximity to Kaliningrad was something else to worry about.

In the end, the accommodation that we could afford and permitted us to house our cats was found in Krakow. We eliminated the option of travelling by train as only women and children were permitted to board. However, there was no restriction on men travelling in buses as long as they were not within the army serving age. But there were no services running from Lviv into Krakow either. We either take an overnight bus to Warsaw and then find another bus or train to Krakow, or our friend could drop us at the border and we could walk into the Polish town on foot to find a transportation into Krakow.

By then we already had a phobia of having to scramble with others. Unlike holiday travelling, where getting from point A to point B could be surprisingly interesting when things do not go according to plan, during a mass exodus, it would be less chaotic when things go according to plan, from A to B, B to C and all the way until we arrive at our destination.

Fleeing as refugees with our cats and belongings was difficult enough when we had to carry our belongings while walking. Changing between public transportation at stations overcrowded with refugees was a scenario we wanted to avoid.

It was more logical to rent a car from the bus station in Warsaw and drive ourselves to the apartment in Krakow. So we decided that we will book our transportation to Krakow once the vaccinations for our cats were completed, luck permitting.

Crossing the Border

AFTER OVERWHELMING REPORTS of attacks on humanitarian evacuation corridors, Russia finally announced safe corridors for evacuation into Russia. There was even a story about an Ukrainian man who found himself being cut off from his parents and girlfriend by the sudden appearance of the frontline. So he drove into Russia and looped 3,700 kilometres across five countries to be reunited with his loved ones living on the other side of the frontline in Ukraine.

Without any car of our own, we were better off not planning anything too majestic. The vet at the clinic was very helpful as she attended to the needs of our cats during her lunch break. We had been lucky to meet very helpful Ukrainians on our journey, it was encouraging to experience the better side of humankind in unexpected ways.

With our cats certified to enter the European Union, we searched for the earliest available bus ride into Warsaw. Just like the emergence of new train routes, trans-border bus operators sprouted like mushrooms after a storm. There were so many operators to choose from but there wasn't one single online platform to coordinate them.

IMPRESSIONS OF AN INVASION

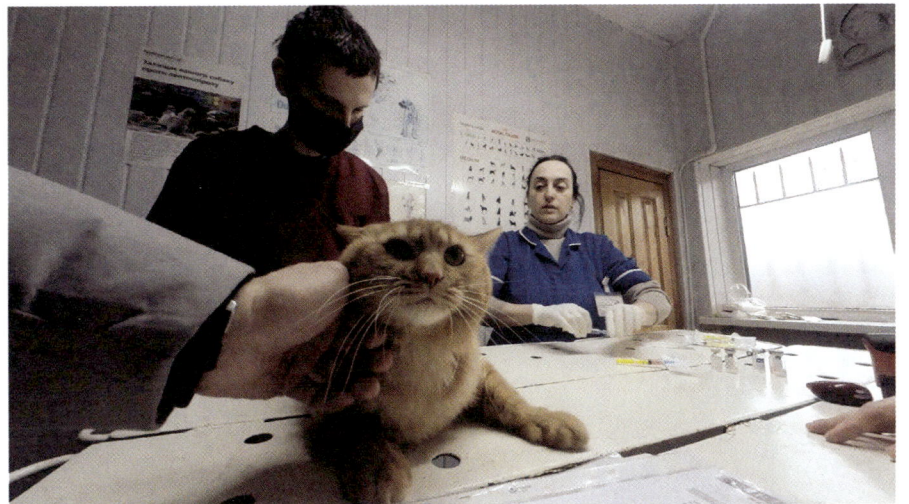

Bolshevik braving his vaccination jab

Natalia had to call them one at a time to verify their destinations with available seats. To make the task more challenging, some operators had been block-booked by charities in advance so that they could give out free tickets. Ironically, some of those charities may not have found enough refugees to fill every trip.

We eventually bought tickets for a bus leaving the next night, and was scheduled to arrive in Warsaw around noon the following day. So I booked a rental car to meet us at the main bus station on the day of our arrival.

Being better rested in our nights in Lviv, we spent our remaining day walking around the beautiful city. Although there was an undeniable ambience about the impending invasion, the solidarity of the people and the place gave the city another dimension to its beauty.

We went to a well-stocked supermarket to buy some food and water for our journey, preparing ourselves for the unknown amount of time we might have to spend crossing the border.

We tried playing with the cats since they would be spending hours inside their carriers for the upcoming journey, but they could sense our apprehension about the unknown and it felt more like they were reassuring us by playing with us.

That night, our friend came over to help us with our belongings and gave us a ride to the central bus station. As the train and bus stations were located opposite to each other, we could see throngs of people lugging all kinds of bags and luggage towards the departure hub.

Everyone looked glum and uncertain. Children were clutching onto mothers or siblings. Some of the elderly were struggling with baggage on one hand and walking aid on the other. The cold of the thawing spring only made everything even more miserable. The only thing missing in this scene was the violin player – or the musician might have already left on an earlier train. Fortunately, there were large tents set up by volunteers at an open area outside the stations providing warm food and heating.

After stopping the car outside the bus station, Natalia went ahead looking for our bus inside the huge parking area. Without any illuminated signage to display its destinations, refugees resorted to the flashlight function of their smartphones and went from bus to bus to check. The scene reminded me of a live concert which the audience were not in cohesion with the music. We unloaded our belongings by the side of the road.

Natalia came back with the good news that our bus was not fully occupied, which meant that she could purchase spare tickets for our cats. It was a huge relief that we did not have to place those pet carriers on our lap for hours.

We bid our friend farewell and thanked him for his effort in helping us. He was apologetic about our accommodation situation in Lviv, but we were so grateful for his help arranging our transportation out of Kyiv.

The time for boarding had arrived and with a heavy heart, we began our departure from Ukraine.

There were only three male adults among the passengers of women and children accompanying several pets. An elderly man accompanying his wife, a lone German national and myself.

The bus conductor went down the aisle performing a headcount of all the passengers, we showed him the tickets for our cats when he reached our row. He told us that we had been lucky with our timing for just a week ago, the passengers were sitting three to a row while the entire length of the aisle were filled with people trying to leave.

Our bus started its engine and departed from the station a little after 9PM. There was no excitement when our excursion commenced. The distance from Lviv to the border was a little more than 70 kilometres.

Knowing that the Russian were targeting weapon supply routes entering Ukraine, we could only hope that we would not be travelling in the opposite direction of those similar routes.

After an hour, our bus stopped by the side of an unlit road and shut down its engine. We were told that there was a toilet a few hundred metres away and that we were to wait at the current location until further notice. We alighted with many of the passengers and tread carefully in the dark. We could see the tail-lights of another bus being parked in front of us. Squeezing through the space between the two buses, we crossed to the other side of the road and followed other passengers walking ahead of us. From the other side of the road, we could see that a convoy of buses had been formed in the middle of nowhere.

I made a mental note to memorise the license plate of our bus as we walked towards a petrol station that was in nearly complete darkness. Natalia joined the two lines of women queuing up to use the toilet while I ventured into the bushes on the other end of the petrol station. I waited for Natalia by the side of the road while watching other arriving buses join our convoy. There was no traffic coming from the opposite direction though.

Together with Natalia, we returned to our bus by crossing the road and walking alongside the convoy. Accents from all over Ukraine could be heard by passengers who had gathered outside their buses to update each other.

We decided to return to our seats as we felt everybody was just as clueless and filled with anticipation like us. We were unlikely to learn anything new and did not want to stand in the cold any longer than we had to.

I had already fallen asleep when our driver restarted the engine. A quick check on my watch told me that we had been waiting for nearly three hours. After a headcount by the conductor, our bus pulled out from the side of the road and joined the convoy of buses heading west.

IMPRESSIONS OF AN INVASION

Departing Ukraine at dawn

We arrived at the Ukrainian side of the border and our bus drove into an inspection lane, stopping behind another bus. Our conductor went down the aisle collecting everyone's passport while we were told to remain in our seats. Some of the children and elderly had to flee in such a hurry that they never had the opportunity to apply for a passport. But drastic times called for drastic measures, as the immigration officers boarded the bus later to verify the passengers travelling without passports. Everyone was permitted to leave the country without issue. We waited until the conductor returned all travel documents, then our bus drove out from the inspection lane and stopped beside an closed duty-free store.

We had a 20-minute toilet break before crossing into Poland. So everyone alighted from the bus to walk on Ukrainian soil one last time with no knowledge of whether we would return. There were a lot of people queuing up to use the toilet. And since I could not find any bush around an area surrounded by security cameras, I decided to join the queue for the toilets. As the number of men and women were very imbalanced, all the toilets was unisex to cater to everybody.

By the time I came out from the toilet, the eastern part of the sky was already beginning to glow with the dawn of a new day. I took one long look at Ukraine before returning to our bus.

The border control of Poland was just one turn away, we had to remain on the bus until a Polish customs officer directed our bus to enter one of the inspection lanes. Everyone had to alight from the bus and carry all our belongings to be processed individually at the immigration counters.

Carrying all our belongings on us, we walked inside the immigration centre together with the other refugees. The Polish immigration officer was slightly bewildered when he saw my Singaporean passport, he did a quick check about the visa requirements and stamped it promptly with a greeting in English welcoming me to Poland. I thanked him and picked up our cats to join the flow of people passing through the customs control.

After we exited the customs control, we were greeted by tables filled with hot coffee, tea, cocoa, snacks and candies. The border control officers were handing out refreshments to everyone like banquet waiters serving at a conference cocktail, except they were wearing bullet vests and sidearms. The Polish were truly sympathetic to the Ukrainians and trying their utmost to help.

Polish and international volunteers offering hot food and beverage to help calm nervous refugees.

Toys and games are a tremendous help for children too young to vocalise their trauma.

Our dominant female – Tiger staring down a fellow dog refugee

Perhaps it was the effect of the sunrise or the relief to be inside the territory of a NATO member country, everybody seemed to be feeling more at ease as we chatted while sipping on a hot beverage and snacking on biscuits. We were ushered back onto our bus as another bus drove up behind ours and began alighting its passengers.

Another headcount was conducted before we moved out from the Polish border crossing. I admired the picturesque farmlands of the Polish countryside as we drove on the highway with signboards printed in Latin alphabets. Turning around to check on Natalia and the cats, I noticed everyone had fallen asleep as the sun rose higher from the horizon. I allowed that feeling of safety to engulf me and felt my eyelids becoming ever heavier.

Arrival Terminals

OUR BUS ARRIVED in Warsaw around noon. But as an unscheduled arrival, we did not get to stop inside the Central bus station and could only stop by the side of a road at a bus stop situated on the motorway opposite the Central bus station.

Everyone dispersed and I crossed the motorway through a long underpass to search for the rental car we had prearranged to meet us the main carpark of the Central bus station. Walking through the Central bus station was a humbling experience when I saw an overwhelming number of Ukrainian families sleeping or resting on the floor of the station. People were huddled together for warmth and support while waiting for help with the relocation to shelters in Warsaw or other cities.

I could tell from the look on the many of their faces that the shock and overbearing agony of being uprooted from a destroyed home had only just begun to set in, now that they had finally reached a place safe enough to start pondering. Due to an oversight of using my Singapore rather than the Ukraine phone number when booking the rental car, we ran into some unforeseen complications which delayed us by several hours.

Unlike popular countries that Singaporeans like to travel, I had encountered numerous situations where the roaming services of my Singapore SIM card were very unreliable. This took place whenever I was in the less popular destinations of my fellow countrymen and women. Because my Singapore SIM card was uncontactable, I failed to answer the messages and phone calls from the rental company and our rental car was no longer in Warsaw.

We did not want to struggle carrying our cats while laden with all our other belongings and chose to avoid public transportation because we knew Poland had waived travel tickets for Ukrainians travelling within Poland. Two Polish volunteers were kind enough to help us with our situation by calling the Polish-speaking rental company to find a solution. They were a pair of animal lovers delivering pet food for abandoned pets inside Ukraine. They recommended that we try our luck at the airport as there were plenty of car rental companies there.

Grateful for their help and the modernisation of our information technology economy, I managed to reserve a car from another rental company that displayed their inventory of available cars online. We booked a car to take us to the airport though a ride-hailing app. The Georgian driver was even willing to drive us to Krakow if we booked the trip on the app as well.

We placed all our belongings onto an airport luggage trolley and went inside the airport terminal building to pick up our rental car, only to stop suddenly at the entrance by a signboard informing everyone that face masks were required for entry.

Ever since the beginning of the invasion on 24th February, face masks had become a completely forgotten requirement for all of us trying to stay sane and alive on a day to day basis. Being jerked back into the sphere of COVID mindfulness was entertainingly jovial to say the least.

Bona fide refugees inside the European Union

Fortunately, I had a few unused facemasks in my backpack left from our snowboarding trip in the Caucasus mountains in January. We slapped on our face masks only to be clapped again by the car rental company when the staff explained their company could not rent the car out to me due to my Singapore driver license – something to do with insurance coverage issues.

I sincerely could not believe that Singaporean drivers had caused that many road accidents on Polish roads for them to create such a clause. Natalia could not rent a car either as her driver license was the old Ukrainian booklet version and did not have the modern identity-secured plastic card. It was just another unnecessary trying disappointment we had to deal with after all the hoops we had already jumped through.

Our journey had always been full of ups and downs and was rarely flat. In fact, when things started to go smoothly, I needed to check if there was any astronomical alignment of celestial bodies. Natalia was too tired to feel desperate and decided to take a trip to the ladies. I just slumped into my Asian squat against the wall while waiting for her outside the toilet.

Staring at the row of car rental companies, they were mostly large franchises with fancy advertisements that I had seen while searching for rental cars on search engines. They had wonderful marketing and user-friendly sites to entice customers to rent their cars, provided they had a driver license which complied with their corporate insurance policies.

Near the toilets was an inconspicuous car rental company with a rather bland looking signboard. I approached the man behind the counter and enquired if I could rent a car from their company using my Singaporean drivers license. He looked up at the keyboard – as in a board where all the car keys were hung – and asked how many days was I intending to rent.

Their rental rates were even more competitive than any of the companies that I had checked online. I concluded that I should not be grateful for all those easily searched companies and user-friendly websites, since we will be charged for those conveniences anyway.

Aftermath

LIKE MANY OF the refugees that made their way into places of safety, I presumed that we would not be immune to some form of PTSD. For me, trauma is something that can only be experienced but not explained.

Cross-referencing Kubler-Ross Change Curve with the various stages of PTSD symptoms, it is kind of like letting a mischievous bartender become the deejay remixing my memories. Throughout the many ordeals encountered, I did not recall any incident that made me feel like I was having the earth collapsing beneath my feet. I can still remember the sensations my body felt when I leapt from a 10-metre diving platform as a kid, my first skydive from a Cirrus low-wing plane or the time when I was caught in a riptide dragging me underwater in Bali.

However, those episodes of staying, surviving and leaving Ukraine had been an adrenaline rush while my emotions remained within the manageable range throughout, all the way since day one until we arrived and settled into the apartment we had rented.

I headed to the supermarket to buy food and water while Natalia was trying to take a long bath to decompress. After grabbing a shopping basket by the entrance, I suddenly stopped in midstride between the fresh fruits and refrigerated diary sections.

IMPRESSIONS OF AN INVASION

I did not know whether it was it due to the abundance of food available, the audacity of people doing their evening shopping in serenity or the guilt and worry for our families and friends back in Ukraine. My eyes welled up and tears begun rolling down my face even though I was not sobbing.

I guessed that I might between the second and third stages of PTSD, and would need to wait until I can begin reviewing these experiences from a third-party's perspective before transcending into a recovery process. I continued in silence while placing items into the shopping basket in autopilot mode.

We like to tell ourselves that everything will return to normal, our ability to adapt and survive will help us to recover and reconstruct our lives. But it is also our ability to adapt and

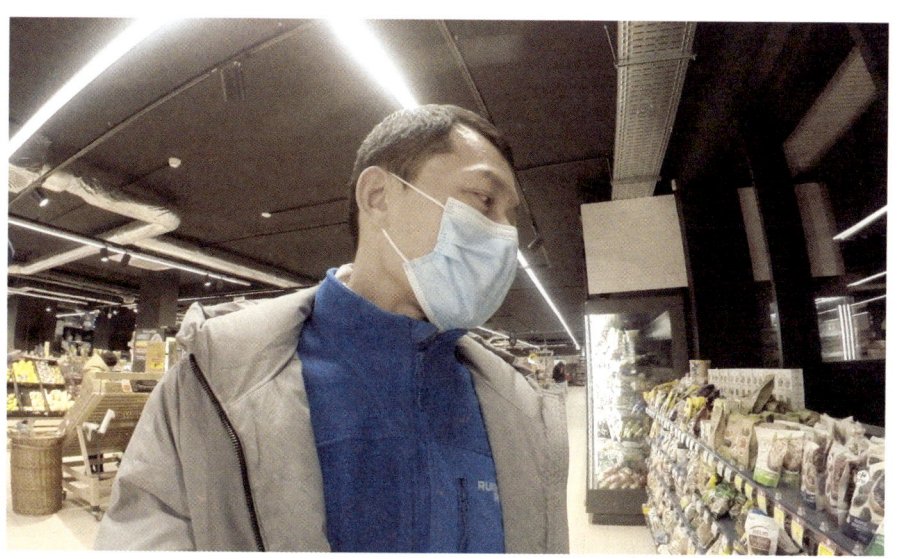

Danger ended as abruptly as it started – the shock was not from the sight but the possibility of seeing it again.

survive during times of duress that allows us to expand our scope of normalcy in order to perform rationally under extreme circumstances.

It seemed like the real challenge for our future is how ambiguous our normal was going to be.

Opposite page:
Normal is whatever we deem it to be, as long we don't become lazy at staying safe and sound.

Drawings from pediatric patients of the Chernihiv Regional Children's Hospital while hiding underground.

AFTERWORD

By the time the manuscript was ready for publication, the invasion of Ukraine had been going on for almost a year.

Having established ourselves into a place of safety in Poland, we started to receive pleads of assistance from several of our friends who were still working inside the hospitals in Ukraine. Supplies and medication were getting increasing difficult to come by as stockpiles were diminishing at an alarming rate and supply routes were under bombardments.

We begun asking around and one introduction led to another. What started out as enquiries about how we might be able to obtain the requested supplies ended up with me inside a truck heading back into Kyiv stocked with humanitarian reliefs while wearing a bullet proof vest. That kick-started my desire to continue helping the Ukrainian hospitals with their struggle.

I hope to be able use part of the proceeds from the sale of this book to provide medical assistance to those affected by the invasion.

IX SHEN

Adjusting the bulletproof vest for better breathing during long drives

Ambiguity of Normalcy

Living in peaceful environments far away from life threatening conflicts, it is quite reasonable to look at the behaviour of someone who just came from a war zone and assume he or she is demented.

But I know now that during those times when life or death becomes an uncertainty, normalcy is ambiguous.

Is it normal to factor in the texture of a cat litter as a purchasing decision? Because when I am dumbstruck by the variety of clay, gel, pine, wheat, grass, corn, paper and tofu cat litter available in a pet store, I will now choose the one that can stop a bullet. Similarly, the housewives in Kyiv today would so naturally discuss whether asphalt or tar made a better Molotov cocktail when thrown.

When the situation gets ever more dire. Our ability to adapt driven by the will to survive will allow us to morph the ambiguity of what used to be normal. Any inability to adapt would just be viewed by the others as abnormal.

Safe and Sound

Coming from a background in media industry, whenever I hear anyone being referred to as a sound person. I would assume by default that the person is from the audio department.

In this internet age of information overload, it becomes very challenging to process and prioritise the bulk of ever changing updates under the intermittent pounding of overhead explosions.

One of the clearest takeaways from my experience during the early days of the invasion is that being safe and sound is more important than food and water.

'Sound' as in 'sound of mind'.

Without being sound of mind, one will not even recognise the body signals for thirst and hunger. When the possibility of not seeing another sunrise becomes real, not going berserk can consume a lot of one cognitive abilities, and that overcomes the primal ones.

As we try to remain in one piece, the absurdism of a war zone will try to amplify the rifts within the conflicts of our conscious, unconscious and preconscious minds.

Holding It Together

When none of the appointments in the calendar application feels important anymore, our concept of time transforms into something else.

All we care about is when this current attack will take a pause and how long that pause was going to last before the next attack begins.

Humour becomes a precious manner in which we can get in touch with our human side. Being able to laugh about how deadly a bottle of pickled cucumbers can be when thrown properly by a *Babushka* against a Russian drone was just one of the many ways we seek respite in any situation where we are under duress.

But I have to admit that the thought of those Russian drone operators' reactions would have been quite entertaining.

I totally get it when I see those dancing videos of the Ukrainian defenders in full combat gear at the frontline. In fact there were several that had gone viral after they posed the "Wednesday Addams" dance challenge to each other.

Everyone is trying their best to persevere with the fight and to win the last laugh.

Barbaric World

Having grown up on a tropical island with decades of near constant economic growth. It is easy to overlook the consequences we paid for the sustainability of growth.

The fundamental of a prosperous trading nation is a secure, rule-based global environment. I was petrified to see fellow countrymen and women being indifferent towards the Russian invasion of Ukraine. I could understand the sense of

IMPRESSIONS OF AN INVASION

Generational feud that time might not heal

non-interference if it were a civil conflict, but when weaponised foreign troops cross international borders without provocation, it is an act of invasion.

Inaction is as good as an endorsement of such behaviour as being indifferent. If Russia were to emerge victorious from this Russo-Ukrainian conflict, a new playbook would have been written for any potential entity who intends to rule by might.

For our future generations of islanders who are lacking in skills of fishing and foraging, a trading nation could only survive in such an environment of the powerful and mighty by double or multiple dealing. Which means that in the event Ukraine is defeated in this conflict, we might need to review the education system to train students to cheat, lie, steal, rob and kill – those would be valuable skill sets in a future where the mighty rules and all bets are off.

Round and About the Looking Glass

One of the things I was looking forward to do when I arrived in Singapore was to meet one of the interviewers that I had been doing correspondent work with while in Ukraine.

It was the radio interview which got interrupted by gunfire. To think that I managed to get out from a war zone in one piece. I was hoping to meet up with the interviewer and relish those exciting moments because he was the only person in Singapore who was together with me in that precarious situation.

While on a trip to the radio station, after a Q&A with another Chinese radio channel, I tried to ask around for the interviewer from CNA93.8FM. My breath was knocked out when I discovered that Eugene Loh had passed away from health issues.

Traumatic episodes always erupt when you are not expecting it. I felt like I was spinning inside the chamber of a revolving door except the door is a mirror. Just barely a year ago, I was the one dodging stray bullets while talking to him on my phone and he was trying to conduct the interview as calmly as he could inside the safety of the studio.

Considering the odds, he should have been the one who is alive. But now it is I who have arrived safely at the studio while he had departed. I could not comprehend how and why our fates were interlinked in that manner but terminated by another.

Having been on the radio airwaves for over twenty years, he will be missed.

Between the Impossible and the Inevitable

Before 24th February 2022, like many others, I thought it would have been impossible for a war to break out in this century.

We have had so many history lessons about the pain and agony of war that it would be impossible to fathom sending tanks and soldiers into population centres with a mission of destruction.

But by now, we have learnt to adapt to the reality of the situation and accepted that it was inevitable.

Between the impossible and the inevitable is what I term as 'crisis'. And during a crisis, everyone panics.

It is our hesitation or reluctance to deal with reality which creates a lot of panic and anxiety that only stretches the crisis in manner which is overbearingly unnecessary.

The sooner we transcend into the inevitable phase, the more cognitive space we can free up in our minds to deal with the situation.

Ideological Bunker

While on a trip to the city of Odesa during the summer of 2022, I took the opportunity to visit my in-laws. Everyone was elated to be able to see and hug one another and for the physical confirmation that we are all still alive and kicking.

Although Natalia's grandmother is bedridden, she is still sharp as blade when it comes to Russia intentions.

We could only prepare ourselves in advance if Natalia's mother and grandmother decisions for a relocation ever rises. Other than that, I understand very well why so many families had chosen to stay or return despite the threats of massive air strikes.

Home is where resilience is.

Summer is also harvesting time and that is when every green thumbing resident proudly tries to outdo his or her neighbour with the yields from their gardens.

Natalia's mother is no exception to the competition – with her family secret recipe of pickling cucumbers to retain that special crunch after being canned for a year.

She proudly showed our would-be-dinner selections as we trotted around her garden.

Generational wisdom had helped every Ukrainian understand the importance of planting during the thaw of spring, and canning and storing produce after summer for the coming bitter winters.

But it still the physical labour of digging wells and underground bunkers of the grandfather generations that amazes me.

Without the machinery of capitalistic convenience, older Ukrainian folks did not have access to excavating machines for personal use during the collective farming days of communist Soviet Union. Natalia grandfather had dug everything himself.

I marvelling at how the efforts of the previous generations are still providing shelter for the children of Ukraine during air strikes in this century.

I hope that this book becomes the closest form of a mental bunker that I can leave for future generations.

Fruits of labour – golden raspberries

Blessing and curse of thick Black Soil (Chernozem) for agriculture, Ukraine became known as the food basket of Europe, resulting in centuries of conquests.

Self sufficency food security

Our forefathers' foresight in building bunkers

Natalia at her hometown – Odesa, Pearl of the Black Sea

ABOUT THE AUTHOR

IX SHEN has had an impressive career spanning across different fields. After serving his national service in 1992, he began his career as a photojournalist with Singapore Press Holdings, capturing stunning visuals that told stories from Singapore and around the world.

He had his debut as an actor in 1995 and was a rising star in the entertainment industry, working on numerous key productions that showcased his versatility and range.

After more than a decade in front of the camera, he switched gears in 2008 to pursue his passion for screenplay writing and quickly found success as a screenwriter, crafting compelling narratives that captivated audiences. This led to him being first Assistant Director on major movie productions in China until the pandemic put a temporary halt to his work.

Ix continues to make a positive impact today – facilitating non-profit medical supplies for hospitals within Ukraine and freelancing as a wartime correspondent, reporting on the invasion of Ukraine and shining a light on the plight of those affected by war.

His determination, dedication, and spirit make him an empathetic and intuitive storyteller with an inspiring experience.